The T Visa Framework

A Guide for Immigration Lawyers Representing Trafficking Survivors

Helen Tarokić, Esq.

Book Cover by GetCovers

Illustrations by Joseba Morales

First edition 2026

Contents

Introduction: Seeing What Was Always There 1

1. The T Visa Framework (The 2024 Regs in 2026) 13
2. The Art of Screening for T Visas (Consultations) 61
3. How Trafficking Appears in Consults (The Hypos) 95
4. T Visa Evidence: Prosecution Not Required 121
5. More Trafficking Scenarios (Now That You're Inspired) 159
6. The Power of the T Visa Waiver (I-192) 195
7. Deportation Defense & Revisiting Denied Cases 225
8. Ethics and Confidentiality 253
9. Social Work Placements in Law Firms 277

Conclusion 297

About the Author 299

Acknowledgments 304

INTRODUCTION: SEEING WHAT WAS ALWAYS THERE

Who This Book Is For

This book is for immigration lawyers who want to get better at their craft — not just the legal mechanics, but the deeper work of truly connecting with clients and uncovering the full story, so they can get the help they want.

If you have ever finished a consultation feeling deflated because a client walked out without a clear path forward, or stared at a file where the legal options felt far too thin for the trauma your client endured, this guide can help you bridge that gap.

It does not matter if you have been practicing immigration law for one year or twenty. The skill of listening deeply enough to recognize when a different legal framework might apply to someone's case is something every one of us is still developing. I am still developing it. Each T visa class I teach, I find some new layer.

What I have learned over nearly two decades of practice is that the cases that initially look like dead ends sometimes are not. Sometimes, a client's history unfolds through better questioning. If you know how to create the kind of trust that makes complete answers possible, you may discover a key fact that changes everything.

Maybe a potential client came in asking about a green card and mentioned, almost in passing, that they will need a payment plan because they still haven't been paid on a construction job they finished. Maybe the person who "took the charges off" a spouse explained the incident all started when a meal wasn't cooked right. Maybe a tech consultant came to see you because their company has been delaying filing sponsorship papers for years. You were not sure what you were hearing, but something told you to keep asking questions.

That instinct is worth developing. This book can help you do that.

The main audience here is immigration lawyers — newer practitioners who are building their practice, and experienced attorneys who are wondering if they might have missed something. Both groups often have the same reaction when they begin to learn more about T visa laws: *I have already seen cases like this. I just didn't see how it would become a T visa case.*

While lawyers are the core audience, I know that advocates, social workers, law enforcement officers, and others who work alongside immigrant communities may find this material useful as well. I want to acknowledge plainly that some readers may be survivors themselves, trying to understand what happened to them or whether there is a legal remedy available.

To every non-lawyer reader: you are welcome here. This book was not written to exclude you. But I do want to be direct — a T visa case is not something to navigate alone. Please use a qualified, licensed immigration attorney for specific legal advice. This book is not a do-it-yourself guide. It is a tool to help people identify trafficking and understand the legal framework around it. This book is not for "notarios" or "legal consultants" who are non-attorneys.

A Note Before We Go Further (Trigger Warning)

This book contains detailed hypothetical scenarios drawn from real patterns of human trafficking. The content includes labor exploitation, debt bondage, sexual violence, domestic violence, intimate partner control, spiritual and religious abuse, cultural coercion, the trafficking of minors, online exploitation, and the trauma of immigration enforcement — including detention and deportation.

You cannot learn to spot trafficking without understanding what it actually looks like. But understanding what it looks like means sitting with some difficult material, and I do not want you to do that without fair warning. You have your own history. That includes survivors and survivor-leaders reading these pages, advocates who carry the weight of their clients' stories, and lawyers who may finish a chapter and feel a quiet dread settle in — wondering whether they have already sat across from someone whose case looked like the one they just read about. That feeling is real, and it matters. It is not a reason to stop, but it is worth naming.

If you are a lawyer and you find yourself with anxiety or retroactive grief over past cases, please know that this book is specifically designed to help you take action — not to assign blame for what you did not yet know. We learn, and then we do better. That is all any of us can do.

A Note on Terminology: "Victim," "Survivor," and "Escape"

Some of the language in this book — and in your case files — may feel clinical, dated, or even harmful when spoken aloud to the person sitting across from you. That tension is real, and it's worth understanding rather than smoothing over.

The law has its own vocabulary, and using it precisely has consequences for your case. "Victim" is not a characterization; it's a legal term. The statute protects a "victim of a severe form of trafficking in persons," and your filings need to establish that your client meets that definition. Likewise, "escape" carries specific weight in T visa case building — it appears in the regulations themselves, including in provisions tied to retaliation against family members. Softening or substituting these terms in your legal documents can blur the very elements you're trying to prove.

That said, what belongs in a brief does not automatically belong in a conversation. Many people with lived experience of trafficking may identify as survivors, not victims — a word that centers their agency and recovery rather than what was done to them. Others reject "escape" because it feeds a rescue narrative in which the survivor is a passive object saved by someone else. These preferences are not universal or fixed: terminology that feels respectful today may not in five years, and individual clients will differ from any general trend.

The practical skill is holding both registers at once. When legal terminology must enter the conversation, explain it: "The law uses the word 'victim' — that's a legal category we need to establish, not a description of who you are." Clients generally handle legal language well when they understand it's the system's vocabulary, not yours. Also, stay current: check in with survivor-led organizations and your client community about evolving language, because this is an area where an attorney's education is never finished.

A Little About Me and Why I Wrote This

My name is Helen Tarokic. I am a licensed attorney and North Carolina Board Certified Immigration Law Specialist. My law office, Helen Tarokic Law PLLC, is based in North Carolina, and I have been practicing immigration law since obtaining my law license in North Carolina in 2006. I work with individuals and businesses across the full range of immigration matters, but humanitarian and victim-based cases — including T visas and U visas — have become a defining part of my practice. I have hosted webinars (Continuing Legal Education or CLE) on T visa practice for attorneys, social workers, and law enforcement, and I have spent years developing screening methods designed to find trafficking indicators during consultations. I did all this because I wanted to get better, but more than anything, I wanted everyone else to get better with me so we could help more people.

I am a first-generation American, a dual citizen of the U.S. and Croatia, and someone whose own family's immigration experience is part of why I do this work. My clients speak English, Spanish, Croatian, Hindi, Gujarati, Urdu, and many other languages. I use a team of interpreters and have built my consultation process around the belief that people deserve to receive legal advice in the language they understand best — including at the very first conversation. If you watch my videos, you'll see I speak Spanish imperfectly. I don't let perfect be the enemy of good, and neither should you.

In 2016, I was anxious about T visa work, too. I had already been an immigration attorney for 11 years and was frustrated because I could not get a local CLE sponsor for a T visa seminar for the better part of the year. Finally, I just applied for my own law firm to become the CLE sponsor in North Carolina and held a seminar in 2017, borrowing a space at our local university for 2 days. I invited people I admired to speak, including people who knew more about T visas and trafficking than I did. It worked! Over time, I began to feel more confident teaching each element of T visas and was exposed to more and more casework and smart lawyers who had big hearts. Since that time, I've received awards, been on the news, and published, but what I am most proud of is hearing when an attorney has won their first T visa.

Now, about this book specifically. In 2024, the federal government issued new T visa regulations that are significantly more favorable to survivors — and as I write this book in 2026, we are watching those regulations be implemented in real cases, in real time. What does that mean? It means that once again, so much is new and up for interpretation, and that is a fresh start. It means what didn't work before might work now. It means you can release the past and work on the future. This book is my attempt to capture what practitioners need to know right now: the updated legal framework, the patterns that show up in consultations, and the strategies that are actually working.

This is not a treatise. Think of it as a guide — a practical, updated foundation for lawyers who are ready to start identifying and representing more trafficking survivors, or who want to do it better than they have been. If something in these pages makes you look at a current client differently or pick up the phone to re-screen someone whose case never quite made sense, then this book has done its job.

Still not sure that you want to start representing trafficking victims? Maybe they are listed in a file collecting dust in a "needs immigration reform" wait list. Maybe they have U visas pending. Maybe they are your business immigration clients. I believe you are already representing many trafficking victims whether you realize it or not, and you just are not filing T visas for them yet.

What This Book Is — and What It Is Not

This is a practitioner's guide built around a specific legal tool: the T visa, which is the primary immigration remedy available to survivors of human trafficking in the United States.

The T visa is one of the most powerful and most underused forms of humanitarian immigration relief that exists. In the right case, it can stop a deportation, provide early work authorization, protect family members, and open a pathway to a green card and eventually U.S. citizenship. It also carries a remarkably broad waiver that can forgive immigration violations — including some that would be fatal to almost any other type of case, such as "false claim to U.S. citizenship."

Many immigration lawyers know the T visa exists. Far fewer know how to use it well, how to spot the cases where it applies, or how to have the kind of consultation that actually surfaces the information needed to evaluate it.

That gap/opportunity to grow is what this book addresses.

What this book does *not* do is start from scratch on trafficking history or policy theory. This book assumes you are ready to get practical. I want you to find the case first. Then you will be inspired to dig more into regulations and templates, team up with a mentor, and file your case.

The Problem with Movies

I want to address the single most persistent obstacle to identifying trafficking cases: the mental image most people carry of what trafficking actually looks like.

Most people picture something cinematic. A woman is kidnapped. She is transported across a border. She is held in a locked room by dangerous strangers. She is forced into sex. She is rescued. The case is obvious. The victimization is clear.

That picture is not entirely fiction. Cases involving violent captivity and physical confinement absolutely exist — and they are every bit as devastating as the film version suggests. Here is what years of practice has taught me about those cases: survivors of violent captivity almost never walk into a lawyer's office to announce it. Trauma does not work that way. Fear and shame do not work that way.

The client who was locked in a stash house may describe it as "a bad time when I first arrived." The woman who was held and controlled for years by an abusive partner may say only that she had "problems with the father of her children." The man who was threatened, underpaid, and told he had no legal rights because of his lack of immigration status may describe it as "a bad job."

If you are waiting for your clients to tell you they were trafficked, you will miss nearly all of them. If a potential client comes in and tells you a story that sounds like only Hollywood could have invented it, take a breath and genuinely listen. Hollywood does not know half of what survivors experience.

This is not a reason for despair. It is a reason to ask better questions. The first step toward asking better questions is understanding that trafficking does not only happen in dramatic, cinematic situations. It also happens in ordinary ones. It happens in roofing jobs and restaurant kitchens, in marriages and motel rooms, on landscaping crews and in convenience stores, in high tech consultancy offices and in high dollar investor conference rooms. It happens to people who still go to work every day. It happens to people whose trafficker is also the person they love.

The following chapters will show you what that actually looks like.

A Note on the Examples in This Book

Throughout this book I use hypothetical fact patterns — "hypos" — to show how trafficking actually appears in legal consultations. These are built from patterns observed across many years of practice, across different industries, relationship types, and cultural contexts. They are not based on any specific client or case. All details are fictional, and several scenarios are deliberately constructed to illustrate how the law applies to particular fact patterns.

I rely on hypotheticals for one reason above all others: the privacy of survivors.

Some of the hypotheticals in this book will feel more legally straightforward than others. A client held in physical captivity with documented injuries and a police report is going to look different on paper than a client who was psychologically controlled in a labor situation where no one ever touched them. That is not a judgement about whose suffering was worse. It is a statement about presenting the appropriate evidence.

I want to name that distinction carefully, because the instinct to rank cases by severity must be tempered. Profound harm does not require visible wounds. Coercion does not require chains. A person can be completely controlled by debt, isolation, fear, or shame — and suffer from years of exploitation without a single photograph or visible scar that proves it. That client's case is not less serious. It is less documented. Those are two entirely different problems, and only one of them is yours to solve.

So, if I describe certain hypotheticals as having stronger documentation or cleaner legal facts, I mean to do so as a practitioner's observation — not a judgment about the human being at the center of the case.

How This Book Is Organized

Chapter 1 lays out the T visa legal framework in practical terms, with particular attention to the 2024 regulatory updates and what they mean for cases being filed and adjudicated right now (in 2026).

Chapter 2 focuses on the consultation itself — the art and the mechanics of screening for trafficking indicators. This includes utilizing familiar allegories to easily teach the mechanics of coercion, the targeted questions that open cases up, the patterns that should make you pause, and the reasons immigration lawyers most commonly miss labor trafficking.

Chapter 3 works through specific fact patterns across the industries and relationship types where trafficking commonly appears in practice: construction and roofing, gas stations and convenience stores, landscaping, smuggling-turned-trafficking situations, domestic violence-based trafficking, and restaurant and hotel work.

Chapter 4 addresses evidence — the "Core Four" components you actually need, why a police-issued incident report is not legally required, how to build a compelling record from the materials your client already possesses, and how to successfully navigate both law enforcement and institutional gatekeepers who reject your legal theories.

Chapter 5 expands the scenario work into additional trafficking contexts: sex trafficking that does not involve money, exploitation of visa holders, trafficking of minors, and spiritual and cultural coercion.

Chapter 6 covers the I-192 waiver — one of the most underestimated tools available to T visa practitioners — and explains how it can overcome bars that would otherwise seem unsurmountable.

Chapter 7 addresses deportation defense: using the T visa process to pause or terminate removal proceedings, responding to a Notice to Appear, and revisiting cases for people with old removal orders.

Chapter 8 covers the professional and ethical dimensions of this work. It addresses strict confidentiality protocols and overcoming practitioner anxiety.

Chapter 9 provides a radical framework for integrating Master of Social Work (MSW) field placement programs into your private law firm to bridge critical service gaps for your clients.

Chapter 10 concludes the guide with a final look at the transformed practitioner mindset, ensuring you leave with a clear action plan for rescreening old files under these new rules.

What I Hope You Take Away

The T visa exists because Congress recognized something important: trafficking survivors deserve immigration protection not in spite of what they have been through, but because of it. The law was designed with them in mind. Our job as lawyers, as advocates, as people who show up for other people in difficult moments, is to use that law as well as it can be used.

If there is one thing I want practitioners to take away from this book, it is this: the cases we are about to discuss are not rare. They are not edge cases or unusual situations that only surface in trafficking-specific law practices. They are the kinds of fact patterns that appear — regularly, predictably — in standard immigration consultations, once you know what questions to ask.

That is not an alarming statement. It is a practical one. It means the skills in this book are not niche skills. They are core consultation skills that every immigration practitioner can develop, and that will improve outcomes across your entire caseload.

That starts with learning to see what was always there.

Let's get to work.

1

The T Visa Framework (The 2024 Regs in 2026)

Why file for a T visa? Get help, heal, legalize immigration status, stop or try to stop deportation, protect family, open pathway to a green card and U.S. citizenship over time.

The Four Pillars: A practical overview of the legal framework (Victimization, Physical Presence, Cooperation, Extreme Hardship).

The BFD Gamechanger: How the 2024 regulatory updates function, including the bona fide determination process, deferred action, and early (c)(40) work permits.

Understanding the Value of the T: Let's revisit what might have been our "go to" case type in the past and what to do once you realize a T is viable as a new primary strategy or a potential plan B (you know I love a good "plan B").

Family member rules and screening: The expansive derivative categories for T visa applicants are very different from U visas and other categories.

Why file for a T visa?

Before we explore what trafficking is, it may be helpful to understand the practical benefits of a T visa application. When someone has been a victim of trafficking, the T visa can be powerful. It can give them a profound sense of psychological and legal safety, and access to resources that are life changing. With an accompanying waiver, a trafficking victim can be officially forgiven by the U.S. government for their criminal and immigration violations. The I-192 waiver approval notice that comes with the T visa approval lists each statutory ground of inadmissibility which was waived (forgiven), so the attorney can double check each disclosure was correctly waived.

Here are a few practical reasons to file for a T visa:

- **Legal protection while the case is pending.** Once USCIS issues a bona fide determination, your client can have deferred action and a work permit — often before the full case is decided. For someone living in the shadows, that alone is life changing.

- **Protection from removal.** A T visa can end deportation proceedings. If your client is in removal proceedings or has a final order, the T visa process gives you tools to protect them while the case moves forward. If a person is in removal proceedings, T visa approval means the immigration judge must terminate removal proceedings. It is mandatory pursuant to 8 CFR § 1003.18(d)(1)(i), which states that the Court shall terminate removal, deportation, and exclusion proceedings when a noncitizen has obtained "[n]onimmigrant status as defined in section 101(a)(15)(T)". Therefore, if a Respondent has received T-1 status, the regulations mandate that proceedings be terminated. For a person with an old removal order, the removal order might be reopened and terminated *sua sponte* by the immigration judge or BIA, after T visa approval.

- **A path to a green card and citizenship.** T visa holders can apply for lawful permanent residence after three years, or earlier if the investigation or prosecution wraps up sooner. This is a real, durable immigration solution — not a temporary band-aid.

- **Derivative protection for family members is often better than what other visas can provide.** Depending on your client's age and situation, spouses, children, parents, and siblings may also qualify for T visa status. For clients whose traffickers used their family as leverage, this protection is not a minor detail. To give a quick example of what might be unreachable for a U applicant, but attainable for a T visa applicant: A 30-year-old man's wife, parents, siblings, and adult stepson may all qualify for T derivative status in certain scenarios. That can happen even if the parents didn't marry before the stepchild's 18th birthday (in a T-1, T-2 spouse, T-6 adult stepson scenario).

- **Faster than a U visa approval.** Currently USCIS can issue 5000 T visas per year. As of July of 2026, it is taking about 32 months to issue a T visa. For U visas, USCIS is still stuck in 2017.

- **Path to U.S. citizenship.** If a T visa winner later applies for and obtains permanent residency (e.g., based on T visa approval), that also opens the door to later on applying for U.S. citizenship.

- **Bring family to the US.** Even adults may be able to bring parents to the U.S. on a T-4 visa. Quick example: Jose was trafficked at his H-2A farming job. The employer had ties to Jose's village in Mexico and threatened to go after Jose's whole family if he blew the whistle. Jose's family lives in Mexico. The T-1 visa may be a good fit for Jose, and Jose's parents may use a consular process for T-4 visas to come to the U.S. and be safe from retaliation.

- **Closure.** If a T visa is approved, you may apply for your client to receive an advance parole travel permit. This often allows the T visa client to visit sick or older family members before they die. That visit may be brief, and the client surely needs to return to the U.S. for ongoing help and stability, but it can provide much-needed closure. After all, many times traffickers isolate and rob a victim of their freedom, so travel can heal wounds.

The T visa doesn't just offer immigration relief. It offers recognition. For a client who has spent months or years being told they don't matter, or that their suffering was invisible or their own fault, having a federal agency formally acknowledge what happened to them carries weight that goes beyond any stamp in a passport.

What Is Human Trafficking for T Visa Purposes?

Before you can spot a trafficking case, you need to know what trafficking actually means in the legal context of the T visa. The definition comes from the Trafficking Victims Protection Act ("TVPA"), Pub. L. No. 106-386, 114 Stat. 1464, 1470 (Oct. 28, 2000), as amended and now codified at 22 U.S.C. § 7101; 8 U.S.C. § 1101(a)(15)(T); id. § 1184(o).

Let me walk you through the main definitions of trafficking that form the basis of a T visa case.

REAL-WORLD COERCION LOOKS LIKE THIS:

THESE ARE NOT JUST THREATS. THEY ARE LEGAL COERCION MECHANISMS.

Labor Trafficking

Labor trafficking occurs when someone uses force, fraud, or coercion to compel another person to perform labor or services. That's the core of it. The trafficker doesn't have to chain anyone to a wall. Force can be physical, but coercion can be the threat of harm against the victim or their family. Fraud can look like a job offer that falsely promises a legitimate salary and decent working conditions, or even green card sponsorship. Coercion is often complex — it's the employer who holds your client's passport, or threatens to call immigration, or docks wages for made-up debts, or isolates workers from anyone who might help them. The combination of those tools is what transforms exploitation into the profitable business of labor trafficking.

Sex Trafficking

Sex trafficking occurs when someone recruits, harbors, transports, provides, obtains, solicits, or patronizes a person for the purpose of a commercial sex act, and does so through force, fraud, or coercion. Commercial sex means something of value is exchanged — money, drugs, housing, anything of value. The force, fraud, or coercion requirement mirrors what we see in labor trafficking: the trafficker doesn't have to use physical violence if they're using psychological control, manufactured debt, or threats instead. A person's safety and life are things of value. Threatening their life constitutes coercion, and leveraging their survival to compel a sex act satisfies the commercial element under the law.

Regarding screening for sex trafficking, don't rule this out just because you don't expect to see it in your client's case or because it's far from your personal or professional life experience. I have been shocked at the results of adding routine questions about 'has anyone offered you money or anything else (such as promises of continued employment, housing, or financial support) for sex?' to my screening tools.

Sex Trafficking of a Minor

When the victim is under eighteen years old, there is no force, fraud, or coercion requirement. None. A minor cannot legally consent to commercial sex, full stop. If someone under eighteen is induced to perform a commercial sex act, that is trafficking.

For minors, it does not matter whether the minor appeared to go along with it, whether anyone held a weapon, or if the minor thought their trafficker loved them. This matters enormously in a T visa practice because clients often don't identify as victims of this type of crime. Minors may have been told (and felt) that they were making their own choices or that they were victims of sexual abuse but not trafficking. Your job is to understand the law clearly enough to recognize what facts constitute trafficking.

Understanding the Legal Framework of the T Visa

The Structure Behind the Protection

When lawyers first learn about T visas, the law can look complicated. There are statutes, regulations, agency guidance, and T Visa Policy Manual provisions that all interact with each other.

But when you step back and look at the structure, the system is actually built around a small number of core questions.

To qualify for a T visa, a person must generally show four things:

1. They were a victim of a severe form of trafficking in persons (so we need to identify the trafficking).

2. They are physically present in the United States on account of that trafficking (usually means they need or are getting some kind of help, like physical or emotional therapy due to suffering from ongoing psychological/physical issues related to the trafficking).

3. They have complied with reasonable requests for assistance in the investigation or prosecution of

trafficking (with certain exceptions) (usually means that their lawyer has attempted to report for them).

4. They would suffer extreme hardship involving unusual and severe harm if removed from the United States (usually means they are getting help in the U.S. but would suffer if those services ended).

Those are the four pillars of a T visa case.

Everything else — evidence, declarations, expert reports, service records, the waiver of immigration/criminal violations and legal arguments — ultimately connects back to those questions.

At first, that framework may seem technical. But over time, most practitioners realize that these legal elements are really just structured ways of understanding a person's experience.

What happened to them?

How did it affect their life?

Why would returning them to another country create serious harm?

Reporting Trafficking: Don't Panic.

One of the elements that often causes the most anxiety for new practitioners involves cooperation with law enforcement.

Many lawyers assume that a T visa case requires a criminal investigation or prosecution.

That assumption is incorrect.

Many potential clients, even though they are told the consultation is confidential, assume that telling the attorney what they suffered will automatically result in a report to law enforcement.

That assumption is also incorrect.

If a person pursues a T visa, the law requires that the applicant comply with **reasonable** requests for assistance from law enforcement. It does not require that an investigation already exists before the T visa is filed. It does not require an arrest. It does not require a criminal conviction. It definitely does not require cooperation with unreasonable requests by police or prosecutors.

In many cases, the reporting process is surprisingly simple.

A report might consist of a short letter or a two-paragraph email describing the trafficking and identifying the victim. The report may be sent to an appropriate agency, such as the Department of Labor, the FBI, or a local police department.

Sometimes the agency acknowledges receipt and does nothing further. That outcome is not unusual. Law enforcement agencies operate under resource constraints and internal priorities that immigration lawyers do not control. They may decide that a case is too old, too difficult to investigate, or outside their current priorities.

In other situations, the trafficking may have occurred decades earlier. By the time the lawyer learns about it, the workplace may no longer exist, the trafficker may have disappeared, and witnesses may be impossible to locate.

None of that changes what happened to the victim.

MOST REPORTS ARE SIMPLE. MOST CASES DON'T LEAD TO ARRESTS.

For T visa purposes, what matters is that the trafficking was identified and reported appropriately.

In other cases the reporting process can be more complex, considering that some law enforcement agencies do not have a victim centered approach. Specific agencies' practices or directives may increase enforcement vulnerability. Also, when screening for T visas some potential clients may fear sharing details about their traffickers or victimization due to fear they would be prosecuted or deported, or due to fears that if an investigation begins the trafficker would retaliate. It is important to remember that there is no requirement to comply with unreasonable requests from law enforcement, and that with proper research and communication there is usually a good trauma-informed agency to report to.

In some cases, applicants may demonstrate they qualify for an exemption to the law enforcement reporting requirement, either due to their age or an exception due to trauma. The T Visa Policy Manual has a lot of helpful information related to the minimum level of reporting required, if any, for a T visa case, and what would be a reasonable request for assistance.

In screening and consultations we discuss and emphasize the confidentiality of the consultation and the risks and benefits of reporting, taking into account what we know about whether an agency is likely to request anything unreasonable from us. This helps protect our clients and allows for informed decisions prior to moving forward with a T visa case. Victims' rights advocacy can help a client navigate the T visa reporting process in a safer way.

Why Law Enforcement Sometimes Gets Trafficking Wrong

Another reality we live with is that law enforcement does not always recognize trafficking immediately.

Some agencies have highly trained trafficking units. Others have limited training or experience with these cases. Everyone has an opinion.

Many investigators are familiar with certain forms of trafficking — such as child sex trafficking — but have less experience recognizing labor trafficking in industries like construction, agriculture, restaurants, or domestic work.

Because of that, lawyers sometimes encounter responses such as:

"This sounds like a labor dispute."

Or:

"We don't see evidence of trafficking."

When that happens, new practitioners sometimes assume the immigration case is over.

But that assumption is often wrong. Law enforcement evaluates cases through the lens of criminal prosecution. Immigration adjudicators evaluate cases through the legal framework governing T visas.

Those are different systems with different standards and different goals.

It is entirely possible for law enforcement to decline pursuing a criminal investigation while USCIS still determines that trafficking occurred, and that the report was properly done, for immigration purposes. For immigration lawyers, the key responsibility is to identify the trafficking, document it carefully, and report it appropriately. What law enforcement ultimately decides to do with that information is only one part of the picture.

Pro Tip 1: Do not assume that someone on a trafficking taskforce understands the definition of trafficking for T visa purposes. Local criminal laws and federal immigration laws are different. Despite a lower burden of proof needed for criminal indictments, some law enforcement officers and prosecutors will not pursue criminal cases they think they cannot prove beyond a reasonable doubt. However, when we are applying for a T visa with USCIS we use the "preponderance of the evidence" standard, which is lower than what prosecution needs for a conviction.

Pro Tip 2: You can report dead traffickers, closed businesses that trafficked your client, and traffickers who are outside the U.S. but are threatening your client, who is in the USA. You don't have to "catch" a criminal. Even if you do not have all the information (perhaps because your client never knew their trafficker's real name, or the address where they were being held), you can still report (the agency can do its own further investigation!) You're the immigration lawyer, not the police.

Pro Tip 3: If you are told this is not trafficking when you report, but you know it meets the legal definition, move on to the next step in your T visa case. Attempting to report is still a report. A report that does not trigger agency action can still be a valid T visa report.

Pro Tip 4: Do not expect that the law enforcement agency will create a proper incident report. You may receive just an email response sometimes. Or no response. It's okay.

How could it be that the trafficking taskforce might not understand your report? For some of the same reasons that many immigration lawyers do not recognize trafficking unless they take the time to learn about how many forms it can actually take. Some law enforcement agencies devote thousands of hours and millions of dollars to anti-trafficking programs. However, some law enforcement officers might get 1 hour of training, or they might have been taught by people who were trained briefly years ago. Some officers are exhausted with their daily beat, just trying to catch criminals in the act for low level crimes. Some officers are receiving direction from above to only focus on money laundering or on violent crimes and have been redirected from trafficking investigations. Sometimes they are looking for state law violations which don't match the federal statute. When you are reporting something they can't easily make an arrest for (nor get their boss's support to ensure full prosecution of a trafficking case), they may not be able to help you.

In most cases we see, there is no trafficking prosecution. Sometimes we might see that a labor complaint resulted in payment for back wages, or that the trafficker was convicted of smuggling, or that the trafficker was deported for a different offense entirely. Again, that does not change the fact that after a proper report, you can help your client move on to an immigration remedy while the criminal justice system does its thing (or doesn't).

Just like we are always learning, you never know where you will find an ally at a Law Enforcement Agency (LEA). I have found that prosecutors' offices often have helpful assistant district attorneys who may be able to talk with you, even if police or the Sheriff's office won't. Sometimes, you may be the one who opens the eyes of a local police officer who had never realized that trafficking was happening in their own backyard.

Think about it like a Law and Order episode. Sometimes the police officers are certain they have a perp but can't get the District Attorney to prosecute. Sometimes the District Attorney wants a prosecution but can't get the evidence they need to take it forward. Your job is not to be on Law and Order. Your job is often solely to meet the minimum legal standard for having reported the trafficking (i.e., notified a law enforcement agency with jurisdiction over the trafficking that a crime is believed to have taken place).

Pro Tip 5: You can choose where to report. Most cities have multiple agencies that would have jurisdiction over a crime. For example, you might have police, the Sheriff, the prosecutor's office, and campus police, as options for reporting, or you might go with a federal agency with broad authority like DOL (Wage & Hour or OSHA) or the FBI. If your client was trafficked in multiple jurisdictions (places), you may have even more options about reporting or getting supporting letters or certifications.

Pro Tip 6: It helps to find former prosecutors or police or federal agents who are now retired from their anti-trafficking career to help guide your reporting practices. They can be brilliant, compassionate people who will get you more help.

Find your community. They also make great expert opinion writers and can help you when you feel like an LEA is gaslighting you. They might also have an idea of who within a certain agency might respond to you better or be able to explain why the law enforcement agency is doing what they are doing.

Pro Tip 7: If emailing a report, keep a 'delivery' receipt for your email. An anonymous tip will be too difficult to connect to your client's case. You can still give limited identifying information and do not need to provide your client's telephone number or overly detailed information with an initial report.

Pro Tip 8: If you FedEx or mail in a letter, be sure to track the package delivery and save it. A package can get misdirected. Tracking numbers don't remain active forever and can be reassigned. You're going to need to prove (both in the T filing and later when adjusting status) that your report was sent to the agency, even if they never took any action on it.

Pro Tip 9: Talk to your client about what level of reporting they are comfortable with. Is their goal to max out attention on the criminal case and see their traffickers put behind bars? Or is it to do the T visa case more quietly and find their justice in the stability that can bring? Listen to your client and let their life goals guide the reporting decisions.

Pro Tip 10: There's a rubric to go over regarding reporting (it is the subject of many CLEs year after year). Keep attending classes on reporting and stay connected with colleagues to stay in touch on current trends. There is a trauma exception for reporting and a few other exceptions. You will want to learn those rules.

Reporting is just one of the four pillars of a T visa case. It can be stressful, but don't panic. You can be strategic about how to report, and my recommendation is to learn about each agency you report to before you move forward. If you think law enforcement makes you nervous, you'd be surprised how nervous you can make law enforcement folks who aren't used to hearing from attorneys. Communication and understanding your role as the immigration attorney can help.

Understanding Physical Presence

Another element that causes confusion for many lawyers is the requirement that the applicant be "physically present in the United States on account of trafficking."

A common mistake is thinking that to win a T visa case, you must show the trafficker brought the victim into the United States against their will. That is simply not true. Often people have come to the U.S. willingly, hopefully, seeking economic or educational opportunities, and they were not trafficked until years later.

Yes, being brought forcefully sometimes happens, and if it did, you can include in your legal argument that the person was physically brought (transported) to the U.S. by the trafficker. But many T visa cases look very different.

Sometimes a person came to the U.S. years earlier for unrelated reasons. The trafficking occurred later, often in a workplace or relationship here in the U.S.

Other times a smuggling situation later evolved into forced labor.

- What the law actually requires is that the person is in the United States because of the trafficking or its aftermath. In real life, that often looks like recovery and stabilization.

- Is the person receiving therapy because of the trauma they experienced?
- Is the person receiving medical care related to injuries suffered during the exploitation?
- Are they stabilizing their life with the help of family, community members, or their lawyer after escaping a trafficking situation?
- Can they not go home because their traffickers have dangerous connections there?

These are the kinds of circumstances that often explain why someone remains in the United States.

Connecting trafficking survivors to appropriate medical care, mental health care, or other trafficking-related services is not just good lawyering (and a compassionate thing to do for someone who may never have had access to these resources before). It is often central to demonstrating why the person remains in the United States on account of the trafficking.

We do not have to pretend a person didn't in some way wish to come to America. Instead we should truthfully explain the reasons the person is still in the U.S. and how those reasons are connected to the trafficking victimization.

The T Visa Policy Manual from USCIS notes: "**C. Physical Presence on Account of Trafficking.** Principal applicants for T nonimmigrant status must demonstrate at the time of application that they are physically present in the United States, American Samoa, the Commonwealth of the Northern Mariana Islands, or at a U.S. port of entry, on account of trafficking. Some traffickers arrange for the entry of their victims into these jurisdictions as part of the trafficking scheme, while other traffickers prey upon aliens who are already in the United States. Aliens already in the United States may have entered lawfully or they may have entered without being admitted or paroled and are unlawfully present. USCIS takes into account any relevant circumstances relating to the applicant's arrival and current presence in these jurisdictions." https://www.uscis.gov/policy-manual/volume-3-part-b-chapter-2

See? It's right there for you.

The T Visa Policy Manual and 2024 regulations have a great section on factors you can explain to show physical presence on account of trafficking. It is good enough that often, if you just go through that list of questions with your client, you will realize you just took down enough notes to build out two pages of the victim/applicant statement for the T visa case.

I may not agree with everything in the USCIS T Visa Policy Manual, but I have it bookmarked on my computer and use keyword searches all the time for ideas about what relevant questions to ask. One attorney I know even had it printed and spiral-bound for her screening team, so they would spend time with it, highlighting what they thought was important. If you're worried about physical presence, read that section in the T Visa Policy Manual thoroughly and repeatedly.

A Practical Rule Lawyers Must Remember

There is one practical rule that every T visa lawyer must keep in mind.

The applicant must be physically present in the United States at the time the T visa application is filed. Because of this rule, lawyers should discuss international travel very carefully with clients once a T visa case has been filed.

If the applicant departs the United States while the T visa case is pending, the application is generally considered abandoned.

That said, in the past, the rule was that a person had to have been trafficked since their last entry to the US, to qualify for a T visa. That rule was not victim-centric, ignored the reality of trafficking for so many people — and it no longer applies! This opens the door back up for many victims whose trafficking occurred many years ago (and may even merit re-screening some clients who came to you in the past!).

Pro Tip about entries and exits: If a person has departed after the trafficking yet returned later to the United States, they may still win their T visa case if you can demonstrate (by a preponderance of the evidence) that they came back and received treatment or some kind of trafficking related help/services related to their victimization, which can't be provided in the home country or last residence abroad. For example, if a person was trafficked 10 years ago, left the U.S. 5 years ago, and returned 4 years ago, and you just now identified them as a trafficking victim and connected them with therapy services for help they really need — that may work for the T visa case.

Isn't it amazing that as immigration lawyers, we can not only combat horrible felony crimes like trafficking, but we can also help our clients with their immigration status? If that wasn't enough, clients might win their cases by receiving help for what they went through. Of course, you need to talk to your client. Talk therapy might not be what they need. Instead, they might want physical therapy for workplace injuries, or removal of a tattoo that reminds them of the abuse. The regulation and T

Visa Policy Manual offer multiple flexible solutions, and you can connect them with professionals who can help them.

Gentle reminder: You're not their savior.

There are limits to how much we can help clients with the emotional and physical effects of the trauma they have suffered. We're their counselors-at-law, but not their actual counselors and therapists. (Your and your team's ability to absorb secondary trauma is also limited.) Also, survivors can be more resilient than you think. But everyone can use a helping hand. If you use the T Visa Policy Manual as a menu for the help your client may wish to receive, it'll help them and the T visa case.

Extreme Hardship

Another key element of the T visa framework is the requirement that removal would cause extreme hardship involving unusual and severe harm.

The USCIS Policy Manual explains that traditional hardship factors may include:

The age of the applicant • *Family ties in the United States and abroad* • *Length of residence in the United States* • *Health and availability of medical treatment abroad* • *Political and economic conditions in the country of return* • *Possibility of other immigration options* • *Community ties in the United States* • *Immigration history*

The T Visa Policy Manual also explains that trafficking survivors may face additional forms of hardship connected to their victimization, including:

Physical or psychological consequences of trafficking • Lack of medical or psychological care in the country of return • Risk of retaliation from traffickers • Risk of re-victimization • Social stigma or punishment for being a trafficking victim • Loss of access to U.S. courts and justice systems • Civil unrest or other threats to personal safety • Economic harm resulting from the trafficking experience

As with many immigration decisions, USCIS evaluates hardship based on the totality of the circumstances.

Pop Quiz: What's one thing the physical presence section, and the hardship section, of the T Visa Policy Manual have in common?

Answer: The use of help in the U.S. to recover from trafficking (e.g., consistent therapy or other trafficking-related help. It's a two-for-one-for-the-win.)

> **Pro Tip:** A couple of sessions with a therapist is not what this is about. An expensive psych evaluation is not what this is about. Your client receiving consistent help prior to and while the T visa case is pending, can make all the difference.

Example: Your client is a survivor of domestic servitude who has been attending weekly trauma-focused therapy through a local anti-trafficking program since shortly after her escape. Her hardship analysis benefits directly from that consistency:

Psychological consequences of the trafficking. Her therapist can document her PTSD diagnosis, the course of treatment, and her progress over time — a longitudinal record no one-time evaluation can replicate. Months of session notes showing symptom patterns, triggers, and gradual stabilization tell a far more credible story than a single expert report prepared for litigation.

Treatment not reasonably available upon return. Because she is in active, ongoing treatment, the argument writes itself: removal would sever an established therapeutic relationship mid-treatment, and trauma-informed care for trafficking survivors is effectively unavailable in her home country. Pair her treatment records with country conditions evidence on mental health infrastructure. An applicant who never sought treatment has to argue hypothetically about care she might need; your client can show exactly what she stands to lose.

Loss of access to victim services. Her therapy is part of a broader web of survivor services — case management, support groups, safety planning — that exists because she is in the United States. Removal doesn't just interrupt one appointment calendar; it dismantles the entire support structure her recovery is built on.

> **Pro Tip:** For some populations — including many LGBTQ+ clients — hardship factors may include fear of persecution in the country of origin. (Be careful, though, not to let this drift into an asylum claim.) On health and medical treatment, screen LGBTQ/H clients for access to HIV care, considering both availability and reliability, since many countries face supply issues. Also assess access to gender-affirming care.

Example: Your client is a transgender woman from Honduras with an HIV diagnosis and treatment regimen. She was subjected to forced labor in the U.S. Her hardship analysis draws on both traditional hardship factors and factors specific to her circumstances:

Medical care not reasonably available. Document her HIV diagnosis and current antiretroviral regimen, paired with evidence that ARV supply chains in Honduras are unreliable and that treatment interruption risks drug resistance and serious illness. Document her ongoing hormone therapy and evidence that gender-affirming care is effectively unavailable to her there. This factor is the workhorse of her claim — a medical need that cannot reasonably be met in the country of return.

Personal circumstances. Country conditions evidence showing widespread violence against transgender women in Honduras and impunity for perpetrators speaks to her personal circumstances upon return. Frame this as hardship upon removal, supported by country condition reports — not as a fear-based protection claim.

Ability and willingness of authorities to protect her. The same impunity evidence does double duty: if authorities are unable or unwilling to protect transgender women from violence, they are unlikely to protect her from re-victimization.

Together, these factors show removal would cause extreme hardship involving unusual and severe harm — well beyond the ordinary hardship of deportation — with her medical needs and the compounding effect of her identity on safety and access to care at the center of the analysis. She may also have an asylum case separately pending where there is overlap, but remember your case for the T visa is documenting hardship according to the T visa law and policy.

The Bona Fide Determination

One of the most important developments in modern T visa practice is the bona fide determination letter, often referred to as a BFD.

As of the summer of 2026, USCIS is taking more than 32 months to issue final decisions on many T visa cases. The timeline keeps moving further and further out.

For trafficking survivors trying to stabilize their lives, that can be a very long time to wait.

The bona fide determination (BFD) process was designed to help address that problem. Today, when lawyers file a T visa case, they usually pursue two types of work authorization.

The first is the work authorization associated with T status itself, issued after the T visa is approved. For the main applicant (T-1), the work permit is under category (a)(16). For family (spouse, child, sibling, parent, adult son or daughter), the category of work permit is (c)(25) and covers derivatives for T-2, T-3, T-4, T-5, T-6.

But practitioners also typically file a (c)(40) work permit application alongside the T visa application, requesting that USCIS make a bona fide determination on the T visa case.

If USCIS determines that the application appears legitimate and contains the required basic evidence, the agency may grant Deferred Action (lawful presence) and an Employment Authorization Document ((c)(40) EAD) while the T visa case is pending. At the time of writing, we have seen BFD work permits issued within a few months of filing (rare), some within 8 or 9 months, many within the 14–16-month range, and some cases where USCIS has not issued the BFD. For some clients, we had to wait until a full T visa decision was issued to get a work permit for the client. We also have had some medical expedites where the processing time was greatly reduced on either the BFD or on the full T-1 adjudication.

Both the deferred action (BFD) (c)(40) work permit, and the T visa, are typically issued for four years. It is challenging but important to take the time to explain to clients why we are applying for two work permits at the same time, each valid for four years and neither guaranteed. We try our best.

The BFD does not mean the T visa has been approved.

Instead, USCIS is essentially saying that the case appears legitimate and that the applicant should receive temporary protection while the full adjudication continues.

For many clients, receiving a BFD is the first moment when their life begins to stabilize. Having the BFD letter in hand is a notification that any removal, exclusion or deportation order is stayed (stopped) while the T visa case is pending. Having a work permit means ability to get a valid social security number and often, a driver's license. It makes it easier to file taxes. A BFD work permit might help the client leave an abusive trafficker by making it easier to rent a new place to live. A BFD approval with work authorization means having a plastic card that functions as an identity document signifying lawful presence. A BFD with deferred action means, of course, hope.

But the T visa needs to be approved, for the person to have valid non-immigrant status (T status) and a pathway to a green card. When a T visa is approved, a work permit signifies that status, and if criminal/immigration grounds of inadmissibility needed to be waived, it is at that point the I-192 waiver will be granted.

> **Practice Tip:** The T visa approval itself is a green, full-sized paper notification valid for 4 years, typically matching the validity dates on the accompanying work permit. Prepare for mail processing fun — USCIS often mails notifications in duplicate, all in separate envelopes, and even the work permit approval notice comes separately from the actual work permit, so be on the lookout for lots of mail and make sure each item is logged into your case management system.

One thing we have found helpful is the safe address rule. As an attorney, we can include a safe address for mail on the G-28 attorney representation form. This allows us to receive all correspondence, instead of the client having to manage it. This also helps with confidentiality and protecting the client's information from family or roommates. (But USCIS sometimes gets it wrong, so have your client be on the lookout anyway.)

An Acknowledgment in the Final Rule

Before the regulation was finalized in 2024, my law firm and others had been pushing USCIS to issue bona fide determinations earlier in the process.

In some situations, the only way to get movement on stalled cases was through federal litigation. Lawyers brought mandamus actions asking courts to compel USCIS to act on long-pending T visa filings. Our ask at the time was to either grant a bonafide determination for each of our plaintiffs or simply make a final decision on the T visa case. In most of our lawsuits, USCIS went ahead and granted the full T visa, and in some, it granted a bonafide determination letter that provided a work authorization option and protection from removal. As a point of history, this meant that for most cases, to get a bonafide determination was not a routine thing, and for each client who wanted one, we had to be ready to sue. Fortunately, a new regulation came out in 2024 that systematized bonafide determinations.

In the preamble commentary accompanying the final rule in 2024, DHS acknowledged that bona fide determinations had been issued in response to litigation. Here is the section I am referring to from 2024:

"By statute, a determination that an application for T nonimmigrant status is bona fide (T BFD) enables trafficking survivors to obtain certain stabilizing benefits, including access to Federal services and benefits via the issuance of Certification letters from HHS, and the ability to obtain an administrative stay of removal...Although an extensive BFD process was codified in the 2016 IFR, such a process has not been implemented in the last decade **outside of litigation cases** due to resource constraints and the inefficiencies of the prior process...After this rule takes effect, on a routine basis USCIS will review an applicant's filing for completeness and conduct background checks to determine if the application is bona fide... Adjudicators will then consider whether an applicant warrants deferred action as a matter of discretion...Applicants may also choose to apply for an EAD at the same time as they submit their Form I-914...This will benefit the applicants because they will be more likely to apply for an EAD simultaneously and therefore be eligible to work sooner than they would have previously." (emphasis added; 89 FR 34864 (April 30, 2024)).

My law firm was among those who worked with litigation counsel to push for bonafide determinations and full T visa approval in cases before the final regulation came out in 2024.

When the final rule formally incorporated the bona fide determination process, it felt like the agency was acknowledging what advocates had been saying for years: trafficking survivors should not have to wait indefinitely for basic protection while their cases are pending.

With the "old BFD rule" we had to show in some way that the client's immigration violations were connected to the trafficking to convince USCIS to issue a BFD (even with a lawsuit). With the "new BFD rule," we don't..!

Sometimes, advocacy works!

Does the New BFD Regulation Work Perfectly?

USCIS has been slow to implement the new BFD rules. In 2024, 2025 and 2026, we had to file new lawsuits to try to expedite some BFD decisions, and other times they have arrived smoothly and quickly.

If a BFD is denied, often that means we have more cause to push USCIS into a final decision. through litigation? Sometimes, USCIS issues the BFD letter, but delays on work permit decisions or issuance. Other times, the work permit has arrived, but the letter is missing. At least once, we saw where the T visa was approved and the BFD arrived shortly afterward, which made no sense at all. A new issue that came up recently has been that USCIS may deny the BFD (seemingly without a reason) and deny the work permit, which then may trigger USCIS's consideration to place an individual in removal proceedings, even if the person has no criminal history. While these may be errors and not trends, it is clear that advocacy for our clients' needs to include a litigation strategy. I have found that knowledgeable immigration attorneys are pairing well with litigators to address these problems and believe we need to fiercely protect and preserve the BFD option for our clients.

Practitioners often communicate about trends, and I have found membership with ASISTA to be particularly helpful, as well as membership with the American Immigration Lawyers Association (AILA). Currently, ASISTA members can schedule what is called a "TA" session — a technical assistance session — where you can get on a video call and confidentially work through the case questions/research issues you are having. Even though we do a lot of T visa work every day, I still reach out to ASISTA because it helps us confirm our strategy or think of new things to help our clients. ASISTA is a national non-profit organization in the U.S. that serves as a legal and advocacy network. They focus on the intersection of immigration and gender-based violence, helping attorneys and advocates who represent immigrant survivors of domestic violence, sexual assault, and human trafficking.

Emailing the USCIS hotline for victim visa cases has helped at times, though it may take days, weeks, or months for USCIS to respond to an attorney's hotline query.

Practice Pointer: When emailing the USCIS hotline, remember to attach a copy of the receipts for the case and your G-28. Be clear that you are requesting supervisor review of a BFD issue, and include your client's name, the receipt/A# information for the case, and your contact information as the attorney of record.

Congressional liaison assistance has also been helpful at times. A congressional liaison is a service provided by a U.S. Senator's or Representative's office to help constituents communicate with federal agencies such as USCIS, the National Visa Center, or the U.S. Department of State. While a congressional office cannot change immigration laws or force an agency to approve a case, it can request status updates, inquire about unusual delays, help resolve administrative errors, and ensure that a case receives appropriate review. This assistance is often most useful when an application has been pending well beyond normal processing times or when there is a compelling humanitarian or emergency circumstance.

If USCIS has not issued a BFD, that does not mean you must immediately infer evil intent. Sometimes it is just a delay. Sometimes it is an error.

Practice pointer: We have won T visa cases despite a "not bonafide" letter, and if you get one of those, the case still has to move on to full, standard adjudication. So if you do receive a letter saying the case is not bonafide, that does not mean your case is, necessarily, incomplete. It may be an error that technical assistance, USCIS hotline help, Congressional liaison, or litigation, can address. You may wish to review your case thoroughly and discuss it again with your client to see if there are any problems previously unaddressed, and from there, push for a final decision on the T visa case or corrective action on the BFD decision.

Potential causes for non-issuance of a BFD letter include things like: not having included properly signed forms, failing to properly sign and date the victim statement, national security issues, or government error.

Screening is Only the Beginning

When lawyers first learn about T visas, the legal framework can feel intimidating. But over time something interesting happens.

Clients will still come in asking about something else, but you will be thinking about T visa screening. Some of them would rather talk about anything else. Some of them, out of fear, will actively hide that they are being trafficked while asking you if their abusive boss can sponsor them, but your alarm bells will go off enough that you will want to ask them more.

A marriage case. A workplace injury. A domestic violence situation. Unpaid wages. A medical deferred action request. You are going to ask to T screen them all.

The trafficking may be hidden inside those stories. Now you're going to have your T visa lenses on, so you'll know what to ask.

Understanding the Value of the T Visa

Who do you talk to first? People you already know. They are the ones who already trust you to tell them the truth. The ones for whom you did not see a remedy for before you put those T glasses on, so you ethically told them, “no.” Those may be the ones you can now re-screen and advise on what may be possible for them.

The First T Visa Cases Already Sitting in Your Files

Let me be direct with you: some of your best first T visa candidates are not new clients. They are people you already represent, or people you represented years ago, whose cases you filed under a different theory because that was the best tool you had at the time.

Rescreening existing clients for trafficking is not an admission that you missed something. It is good lawyering. The law has changed. Your skills have grown. Sometimes the client simply was not ready to tell you the full story the first time around.

Here are some case types worth a second look.

The VAWA Case with a False Claim to Citizenship

VAWA — the Violence Against Women Act — protects abuse victims who are married to U.S. citizens or lawful permanent residents. A standalone I-360 self-petition under VAWA can sometimes result in deferred action, giving the client temporary protection from removal. But deferred action is not a green card.

If your VAWA client made a false claim to U.S. citizenship at any point — like working with a U.S. citizen's identity — they are likely barred from adjusting status to permanent residence. The bar is harsh and the exceptions to a false claim trigger for VAWA purposes are narrow and limited.

But domestic violence is often the mechanism through which trafficking happens. A controlling partner who forces a spouse to cook every meal, clean the house as though it is a commercial operation, and submit to sex, all under threat of violence or deportation has, in many cases, created a situation that meets the legal definition of severe trafficking. Coercion does not need to look like a cage. Sometimes it looks like a marriage.

If that is what your VAWA client experienced, the T visa is worth exploring as an additional pathway. The I-192 waiver that comes with the T visa process can cover the false claim to citizenship ground of inadmissibility. Upon T visa approval and eventual adjustment of status under the T visa pathway, your client may have a road to permanent residence that the VAWA case alone cannot offer.

Do not let a false claim bar be the end of the conversation. Ask about the circumstances surrounding the false claim to U.S. citizenship. You might find the trafficking story right there. Like an uncle who forced them to work off a coyote debt with those papers. It doesn't have to be connected to the trafficking to be waived, but often there is important information connected to the false claim. Rather than cringing when you find a false claim and thinking that there is no hope for your client, consider it a flag for a T visa screen, and put on your thinking cap.

The Asylum Case Involving Gang Recruitment

Asylum is viable for some clients fleeing gang violence. There are risks and challenges to discuss with your client if they are pursuing asylum — immigration court referrals, a judge, cross-examination, a government attorney trying to poke holes in your case in an adversarial proceeding. Even strong asylum cases can be emotionally difficult, especially if the case goes to trial and the client feels attacked on the stand. This doesn't mean that asylum (affirmative or defensive) is not worth pursuing, and it does not mean T visa filings are stress-free, but it means considering the T visa as an option is important, too.

Consider a client from Honduras who fled after a gang tried to recruit him. He made it to the United States. Since arriving, the gang has sent messages trying to re-recruit him here and has threatened his family back home as leverage.

That recruitment attempt — particularly when it involves threats, coercion, and demands for involuntary service to the organization — can meet the definition of trafficking. Gangs that use force, fraud, or coercion to compel someone into membership or service for labor or commercial sex are trafficking. The fact that the client is in the United States while being targeted does not disqualify the claim. It may actually support the physical presence element.

File the asylum case if it is appropriate. But also screen carefully for the T visa. A plan B is not a sign of weakness. It is a "give it all you've ethically got" strategy.

The U Visa Client Who Was Never Fully Screened

This one comes up constantly in immigration law firm practices.

A client sends a copy of a police report. Armed robbery, felonious assault, something violent that happened to them at their workplace. A U visa certification gets signed. The case gets filed. The client settles into the wait, which as of now could stretch more than 10 years or even 20, for a final decision, (unless a law is somehow passed to increase the number of available U visas).

However, did anyone ever ask about the job where the client was assaulted?

Because here is what I sometimes find when I go back and ask: the employer was docking wages for mistakes. The client was not allowed to leave the floor for bathroom breaks. The employer told them they ought to be grateful for the job since they were "illegal." The robbery happened easily because the client was forced to work alone in an unsafe store with no security measures.

That employer's conduct (wage theft, physical confinement, threats based on immigration status) may constitute labor trafficking. The T visa case may be sitting right on top of the U visa case, completely unrelated to the robbery, or directly connected to it.

A client may choose to pursue both cases simultaneously or file one after another. A pending U visa generally does not preclude a T visa filing. Screen those U visa clients for T visas. Just keep in mind that there are also rules related to adjudication, meaning usually once the T visa case is approved, the U visa case will be closed out as unnecessary (or vice versa). I would also ask people to resist the urge to delay rescreening existing clients in search of new clients. Current clients may have made an important investment in a U visa case, but they likely would want to know if there were an additional option.

If pursuing both a U and T visa, remember to cross-check the files for any inconsistencies in data entry or supporting documentation that need review, discussion, or clarification.

Also, for a U visa case, a U visa certification (I-918 Supplement B) is needed, but for a T visa case, a police/law enforcement certification is not required. An attorney may not be thinking of this when only wearing U visa glasses.

WHAT HAPPENS WITH U-VISA-ONLY-GLASSES.

Rescreening Military PIP and DACA and Medical Deferred Action cases

Military parole in place (PIP) gives certain noncitizen family members of service members a temporary foothold in the United States. DACA gives childhood arrivals temporary work authorization. Neither program offers a guaranteed path to permanent residence. Both are subject to political instability and litigation risk that you cannot control.

If you have clients in either category, run through your trafficking screening questions. Not because every military PIP or DACA client has been trafficked — of course they haven't — but because some of them have, and because those clients deserve to know whether a more durable immigration option exists.

Once again, you may pursue your T visa before, alongside, or after, a DACA, Military PIP, or Medical Deferred Action filing.

On my law firm's website, we have a section on Medical Deferred Action. We get a lot of inquiries about it, but often find that the children's medical situation is so dire that it makes it easy for employers to traffic the parents. The parents are so terrified of what would happen if they were deported and unable to care for their child with a rare syndrome or cancer, that they are easily coerced. So rescreen those cases.

DACA holders (the Dreamers) were brought to the U.S. as young kids. They often had little control over their lives. Did you ever screen them for a T? Many DACA holders have been filing their DACA since 2012. They renew every two years without going through a comprehensive consultation with T screening for what has since happened at their jobs, in their relationships, etc. We want to avoid being on autopilot with DACA renewals. Explain to clients or potential clients why screening or re-screening for a potential humanitarian option is important. It's been about 14 years since the DACA program started, and you may wish to explain that during that time, the T visa laws have changed and expanded eligibility such that what a DACA applicant was told in 2012 might be different if rescreened in 2026..

Military PIP cases are ones I find challenging to screen because some people are 100% certain they qualify for a green card. They think everything will go smoothly because they are married to a U.S. citizen and believe America would not reject them after all they've done for the country. It's often after a PIP is denied that they come seeking a second opinion. I encourage them to talk with us through a T screening.

Rescreening "Visa Overstay" Situations

Resist the urge to tell a client on a visa overstay that they should come back after they've found "The One" (who should also be a U.S. Citizen). Ask them more questions — why did they overstay? What happened to them when they did? What jobs did they have and which was the worst one? Find out what went sideways, and you might find out they've been T visa eligible all along. It makes me sad when someone says that they've been in consult after consult, none lasting more than 30 minutes, only to be told to come back if their romantic life improves. There are so many more questions to ask to see if you can help them now.

Now Take Out a Piece of Paper

Write down the names of clients who keep you up at night. The people with the hard cases, the lost appeals, the people you still think about years later. The client whose 42B cancellation of removal you litigated beautifully and still lost. The person you so badly wanted to help in a consultation but sent away telling them they had no options.

Write their names down, or their initials, or just the case type if that is easier.

Now think: what kind of case did they have? What grounds did you pursue? Was there a controlling partner, an exploitative employer, a situation involving force, fraud, or coercion?

Without immigration reform on the horizon, a T visa may open a door you thought was permanently closed. Reaching out to check is not raising false hope – It is doing your job.

Part of my role here is to motivate you. For years now, I've been hearing back from people who attended our classes saying they are so glad they reached back out to an old client to see if they might come back for a new consult and T screening. We don't promise or guarantee anything, of course. We just say that it's time for a new conversation and we apologize in advance, it will be a lot of questions. We do this systematically.

List four current clients you worry about a lot, and what it is that worries you.

1.
2.
3.
4.

List three consultations you remember where you could not find a viable path forward, where you think more questions can be asked.

1.
2.
3.

List three former clients you plan to contact after reading this book and what made you think of them now.

1.
2.
3.

Now look at those names, or initials, or case descriptions.

What is one thing you can do in the next five minutes to move toward getting them all rescreened?

Maybe it is drafting a two-sentence email to your paralegal. Maybe it is putting a sticky note on your monitor. Maybe it is texting yourself as a reminder. Something small. Something real. Something that costs you five minutes and no money.

Write it here:

Now write what you are afraid of.

Are you afraid of raising hope that doesn't pan out? Afraid of reopening a file you closed and grieved? Afraid the client will be angry you didn't ask sooner? Afraid of learning something hard about what they went through?

Write it down. Nobody is grading this.

1.

2.

3.

What might get in your way?

A full docket. A difficult partner. No one on your team trained to do trafficking screens. Your own burnout. Your own history. Be honest here, because whatever lands on this line is what you are actually managing, not just the theoretical obstacle:

What will you do to make sure this actually happens?

Accountability partner. Calendar block. Fee agreement template ready to go for the rescreening consultation. A trained paralegal on standby. Taking a CLE to learn more about T Visas. Reach out to a fellow attorney who seems passionate about inclusive T visa work. Whatever your version of infrastructure looks like, write it down.

1.

2.

3.

Now calendarize it.

Open your calendar right now. Block time — even thirty minutes — specifically for this task. Name the block "T Rescreen Review" or "Follow Up — Ten Files." Whatever works for you.

Done? Good. Now you know the value of the T a little better because you have real people in mind, and a plan to help them.

The Derivative Multiplier: Protecting the Family

The T visa outpaces many other forms of humanitarian relief because of its expansive derivative benefits. Throughout this book, you will see hypotheticals where an adult brings in a parent, or where a sibling is protected. This is not magic; it is a statutory mechanism.

To use this mechanism effectively, you must understand the age divide, the retaliation exception, and the waiver trap.

The Golden Rule of Derivatives First, recognize the baseline: derivative beneficiaries are not required to prove they were trafficked. They do not have to comply with law enforcement, and they do not have to prove physical presence in the United States on account of trafficking. They derive their status entirely from the principal applicant's (the T-1's) eligibility and are petitioned for on Form I-914A. *(Note: If the family member was also exploited and is inside the US, you should screen them for their own standalone T-1 case, which could provide stronger independent protection).*

The Age Divide Eligibility for standard derivative status hinges on the principal applicant's age at the time the T visa is filed.

If the T-1 principal is **under 21 years of age** at the time of filing, they may petition for their:

- Spouse (T-2)
- Children (T-3)
- Parents (T-4)

- Unmarried siblings under 18 years of age (T-5)

Note that a young, married T-1 applicant who is still under 21 can get all of these relatives included. Marrying as a T-1 who is under 21, doesn't prevent the standard derivative T-4/T-5 parent or sibling applications, for example.

If the T-1 principal is **21 years of age or older** at the time of filing, the standard derivative list shrinks at first glance. They may generally only petition for their:

- Spouse (T-2)
- Children under 21 years of age (T-3)

Because of this statutory divide, identifying a potential T visa client who is 20 and approaching their 21st birthday requires immediate triage. Aging out severs their ability to easily sponsor their parents and minor siblings, unless...

The Retaliation Exception

Hypo: What happens when your client is a 30-year-old man, but his trafficker has threatened his parents and siblings back in his home country as leverage?

The statute contains a critical exception to the age limits above. Regardless of the T-1 principal's age, you can petition for certain extended family members if you can demonstrate a "present danger of retaliation" as a result of the survivor's escape from trafficking or their cooperation with law enforcement.

Under this retaliation exception, an adult T-1 may petition for additional derivatives such as:

- Parents (T-4)
- Adult or married sons and daughters (T-6) if the T-1 has a T-2 spouse.
- Stepchildren (T-6) even if the T-1 married the T-2 spouse after the stepchild's 18th birthday.
- Adult siblings of the T-1 (i.e., your client's adult brother or sister), via T-6 category, if you also had a T-4 parent case under the retaliation rule.

This is how an adult can petition for an adult stepson, or how an adult survivor brings parents to the U.S. to escape danger of retaliation from traffickers. It requires an evidentiary showing of that retaliation risk — such as threatening text messages, sworn declarations, or police reports from the home country demonstrating that the trafficker's network is acting on its threats. Sometimes we will use an expert opinion letter from professionals who have been trafficking investigators, who concur that the risk of retaliation never really went away, despite passage of time.

The Filing Mechanics and the Waiver Rule for Derivatives
Filing for a derivative is initiated using Form I-914, Supplement A (i.e., Form I-914A). As with a T-1 case, normally for those in the US, there will likely be an I-765 and I-192 filed, or if the derivatives are out of the US, then the I-765 would not be filed until they enter in T derivative status.

The T-1 principal's I-192 waiver does not magically cover the whole family.

Every single derivative beneficiary should be screened independently for inadmissibility, and you need to run a conflict check before you offer consultations for derivatives. If your client's spouse is living with them in the United States and entered via visa fraud, that T-2 spouse needs their own Form I-192 waiver for prior misrepresentation. If a T-3 teenager was caught with cannabis under a controlled substance schedule, they need their own Form I-192 waiver. Do not submit a Supplement A for an inadmissible derivative without an accompanying I-192, or you invite a denial. You should analyze and cure every derivative's inadmissibility just as rigorously as you do the principal's inadmissibility. You will also need to set up your internal drafting and file review protocol to loop back to the T-1 applicant's disclosures of inadmissibility grounds on their application, if the derivatives tell you the T-1 applicant helped them get smuggled to the U.S. In other words, if a new ground of inadmissibility becomes apparent when preparing a case, it must be disclosed. Having a system in place to cross-check files to ensure full and ethical disclosure for each applicant will help avoid gaps and discrepancies.

The T visa Policy manual has more information on derivative beneficiaries, but here are a few statutory problems we have run into:

1. It seems that a T-1 applicant who is a parent cannot file a T-6 for an adult child, without the T-1 having a T-2 spouse. Example: Trafficker is the spouse of a woman whose daughter was also threatened. The daughter is over 21. The T-1 applicant has not divorced the trafficker yet nor remarried, so there will be no T-2 spousal case. We cannot do a T-6 for the daughter under my reading of the law. This is a statutory drafting issue that omits a benefit for those who are effectively single parents of adult children, though they can sponsor their minor children (e.g., T-3 derivatives). In this hypo, the T-1 applicant may sponsor a child under 21 who is unmarried for T-3 status, but not

her adult daughter. If she were married and filed a T-2 spousal case, she could include the T-6 petition for her daughter who is an adult.

2. T-1 applicant wishes to bring in their siblings who were threatened in India, on T-6 visas. There is a clear danger of retaliation to the siblings since the smuggler who orchestrated the sex trafficking has been harassing both the T-1 in the U.S. and the potential T-6 siblings in India. The parents of these siblings are both deceased. There is not an option to do a T-6 petition for the siblings, because we lack the T-4 parent option. If at least one parent were alive and able to do a T-4 case, the T-6 siblings could be sponsored.

Still, there are a lot of expanded derivative case options available in the T visa context, and it is worth spending time reviewing the T Visa Policy Manual for them. This section is just a start.

Expansive Derivative Exercise

Your client is in removal proceedings. She is single, unmarried, and age 32. She has no children. You have screened her thoroughly, and she was never trafficked. You cannot find an asylum or EOIR-42B option for her. Her parents are undocumented and live in North Carolina. OCC has already refused prosecutorial discretion. What T visa option may you find for your client in removal?

If one of the parents has been trafficked, then you may have a T-1 (e.g., mother), T-2 (e.g., father), T-6 adult child (e.g., your client in removal) case.

Ask about siblings. You find out her sister was abused for years by an intimate partner to the level of it being trafficking.

Perhaps the abusive partner also physically threatened or verbally harassed the parents, giving rise to a present danger of retaliation. Consider a T-1 for the sister, a T-4 for the 2 parents in North Carolina, and a T-6 sibling case for your client in removal.

The T-6 category is a bit odd in that in the above situations it covers your client either as an adult child or a sibling, and a "middleman" derivative is needed for her to be a derivative as well.

Practice Exercise

Consider the clients in your own files who faced removal proceedings and accepted voluntary departure as their only option.

Think through those cases now:

Do any of those clients have a parent, sibling, spouse, or other family member who may have experienced trafficking? Write down a few cases to look at.

1.

2.

If the answer is yes, or even possibly:

Is there a pathway to T derivative status for your former client through that family member's T-1 case? Write down your thoughts and questions.

1.

2.

The T visa's derivative structure rewards exactly this kind of backward glance through your files.

2

THE ART OF SCREENING FOR T VISAS (CONSULTATIONS)

How Trafficking Appears in Consultations

One of the biggest mistakes lawyers make when learning about trafficking is assuming that the exploitation will look dramatic. People tend to imagine kidnapping rings, organized crime networks, or situations where the crime is completely obvious the moment the client begins speaking. In reality, trafficking cases rarely look like that during an immigration consultation. Instead, they appear disguised as other legal issues, such as family petitions, workplace disputes, domestic violence cases, or removal defense situations.

If trafficking always presented itself clearly, immigration lawyers across the country would be identifying these cases every single day. Consultations would simply begin with a client sitting down and stating that they believe they were trafficked and need legal help. But clients almost never use those words because they are traumatized, terrified of deportation, and usually do not view their own survival through that legal lens. Your job as an immigration practitioner is to listen past the surface of the consultation to hear the coercion hiding underneath.

> ***The most important skill in trafficking screening is asking the next question.***

Why Immigration Lawyers Miss Labor Trafficking

Immigration lawyers frequently miss labor trafficking because we are trained to quickly look for cases through a very specific, narrow lens. We are incredibly good at spotting U visa cases, so we constantly scan for police reports, physical assaults, and signed law enforcement certifications. When a client comes in without a police report, or when they describe a problem that sounds like a messy labor dispute, we often turn off our humanitarian screening radar and conclude there is no case. We sit back and wait for clients to self-identify as victims of a severe crime, completely forgetting that people who have experienced trauma rarely offer up their most deeply guarded secrets to a stranger.

Trafficking survivors are actively conditioned by their abusers to believe that no one can help them and that they have no legal rights. They are told that if they complain about their working conditions or their abusive partner, they will be the ones who get arrested and deported. Because of this intense psychological conditioning, they do not walk into your office eager to report a crime. They walk in hoping you might magically find a way to get them a work permit or defend them in immigration court, so they can keep surviving. To uncover the trafficking, you have to transition from passively waiting for a client to volunteer information to actively screening every single person who walks through your door (or in our office, who calls — we do screenings and consultations by phone). You may find out the person wanted to get a work permit to escape the trafficking but did not know that there are work permits for people who are being trafficked.

Finding the "Critical Markers"

Uncovering a trafficking narrative requires you to ask the right kinds of questions during the consultation. You are looking for "critical markers" — those small, revealing details that indicate someone was subjected to force, fraud, or coercion. To find them, use open-ended questions that focus heavily on money, fear, and control. You want to invite the client to tell their story without putting words into their mouth. That protects the integrity of their eventual declaration.

Instead of asking if they were a victim of human trafficking, you ask who organized their travel to the United States and how they paid for the journey. Ask who decided where they lived, who controlled their transportation to work, and whether they were ever required to hand over their paycheck to someone else. Ask open-ended questions about what would have happened if they had refused to go to work or tried to quit their job. When you structure your screening around themes of control, the client may share indicators of coercion that form the legal foundation of a T visa case.

Patience is key. If you try to hurry this up, it won't be productive. If you're running out of time in a consult, you may want to schedule the potential client for another session where both of you can focus more. Knowing that you care to have the conversation fully will mean a lot.

One retired FBI agent who spent decades working on trafficking cases gave me a new perspective on rushed consultations, teaching me that we should also look at this problem from the survivor's perspective. For survivors who have experienced severe trauma, they could be hoping the consult ends quickly because they do not want to disclose the sexual abuse or other painful details, especially if there is something they have never told anyone before.

Challenging the Client Without Cross-Examining

While you must be gentle and trauma-informed, there will be times during a consultation when you have to challenge your client's initial narrative. Clients may minimize their abuse because they have normalized it, or because they do not understand the questions you are asking. They might tell you that their employer treated them fine, or that they never experienced any problems at their restaurant job, because they think you are only asking about whether they were literally locked in a cage or physically abused.

For example, a client might sit in your office and swear that they "never had any problems at work." But as they are talking, you notice severe, raised hot oil burn marks covering both of their arms. That visual evidence completely contradicts their statement that everything was fine. In a situation like that, you may gently push back and ask them to explain the scars. You might find out that the employer refused to provide basic safety equipment, made them work the fryers at a dangerous pace, and threatened to fire them (unlawfully) if they stopped working to seek medical care for the burns [coercion for the purpose of involuntary servitude]. If you do not challenge the initial "everything was fine" narrative, you will completely miss the abuse of the legal process [coercion] and the involuntary servitude hiding right in front of you.

The "Is Everything Trafficking?" Moment

There is a moment that many practitioners have after they have been doing this work for a while. After they have learned the indicators, sharpened their screening questions, and started seeing trafficking patterns in cases that once seemed like something else entirely, they suddenly feel overwhelmed. This moment usually arrives without warning, somewhere in the middle of a consultation, and it sounds something like this: **Is everything trafficking?**

It is a completely fair question, and it deserves a serious answer. The answer is no, not everything is human trafficking. Difficult working conditions are not always trafficking. A toxic relationship is not automatically trafficking. Part of developing as a T visa practitioner is learning how to calibrate your analysis so you can recognize genuine indicators without seeing them everywhere.

The fact that you are asking the question at all means your screening lens has expanded in exactly the right direction. Broad screening does not mean treating every case as a T visa case; it means identifying possible trafficking indicators and asking enough follow-up questions to avoid missing a viable case.

The temporary discomfort of asking yourself, "is this trafficking?" is a far more manageable problem than the silence of never asking the question at all. As your practice grows, your calibration will naturally improve, and you will learn how to weigh what you hear and know when a pattern of facts officially crosses the legal threshold into human trafficking.

Throughout my decade of teaching CLEs on T visas, I've observed that no matter how much time we spend on the "force, fraud, or coercion" concepts and no matter how much time we spend looking at the charts that have been made to try to break down what trafficking is, a lawyer won't be a good screener until they understand the stories, fact patterns, hypos, and archetypes. We have to have something to recognize. So, we're going to start with story time, and what better way to begin than with fairy tales?

Fairy tales serve as a bridge into the heavy industry-specific hypotheticals and help teach the legal elements of force, fraud, and coercion.

Once Upon a Crime: Using Fairy Tales to Understand Trafficking

Lawyers get so bogged down in the technical terminology of the Trafficking Victims Protection Act that they may miss the fundamental human dynamics of power and control. To break through that barrier, I like to use stories that everyone knows to demonstrate these legal elements. Fairy tales are fundamentally stories about vulnerability, exploitation, and survival. For example, in Hansel and Gretel, the witch tricks the children into going into her home (taking advantage of their vulnerability) and then forces them into domestic servitude. The witch then verbally abuses the children for having eaten candy that she actually set out to lure victims to the home.

If you look closely at the fairy tales, many of them are actually cases of severe human trafficking. By analyzing these classic stories through the lens of modern immigration law, we can practice our screening skills and identify the prohibited actions, the means of coercion, and the exploitative purposes that USCIS adjudicators are looking for in a T Visa case.

Once you learn how to spot involuntary servitude or debt bondage in a fairy tale, it becomes much easier to recognize those exact same legal elements with real clients. Let us look at more classic examples and translate them into the real-world scenarios you might actually encounter in your law firm.

The "Perform or Perish" Trap: Rumpelstiltskin

If you recall the story of Rumpelstiltskin, the trouble begins when a boastful miller lies to the king, claiming that his beautiful daughter has the magical ability to spin ordinary straw into pure gold. The greedy king immediately brings the young woman to his palace [transportation and obtaining her labor], locks her inside a room filled with straw [harboring], and hands her a spinning wheel [demanding economic service]. The king explicitly tells her that she must spin all of the straw into gold before morning, and if she fails to do so, she will lose her life [threat of severe harm]. The terrified girl sits in the locked room weeping because she obviously has no idea how to perform this impossible task, which is when yet another abuser appears — the magical Rumpelstiltskin. He appears to exploit her desperation.

From a legal perspective, the king in this story is a human trafficker. He has obtained, transported and harbored the miller's daughter in a locked room for the purpose of involuntary servitude or slavery. He is using the ultimate form of coercion — the explicit threat of death — to make her perform labor that she cannot escape.

Later in the Rumpelstiltskin story, the king has married the miller's daughter. She is now the queen and has given birth to her first child.

> **Pro Tip:** Marrying or having a child does not negate the labor trafficking but rather opens the inquiry further as to whether there were also coerced or forced sex acts.

Rumpelstiltskin returns to the queen's room to claim the baby as payment for spinning the straw into gold. He tells her that she can only keep her child if she is able to guess his true name within a three-day grace period. After the queen sends messengers far and wide to help her, one messenger overhears Rumpelstiltskin dancing around a fire in the woods and singing that his name is Rumpelstiltskin. When the queen finally confronts him and speaks his true name, he flies into a furious rage and runs away defeated.

This dramatic ending illustrates the power dynamics of extortion and child-related coercion that we see every day in human trafficking cases. In our practice, traffickers frequently hold a victim's child over the victim's head as leverage to prevent them from escaping. They might threaten to physically take the children away, report the parents to child protective services, or refuse to let the victim reunite with children left behind in their home country. Just like Rumpelstiltskin demanding the queen's firstborn as his payment, these abusers use the victim's most precious vulnerability to maintain control over their labor or commercial sex services. This story also shows us how more than one person may take advantage of a person's vulnerability to exploit them.

We can translate this into a real-world hypothetical about a domestic worker who is being extorted. Imagine an undocumented mother who is forced to work around the clock as a live-in nanny and housekeeper for an abusive employer. The employer constantly threatens that if she ever tries to quit her job or complain about her unpaid wages, the employer will call immigration to have her deported and will personally ensure her baby is thrown into the state foster care system. The mother is completely terrified and stays trapped in involuntary servitude because she genuinely believes the employer has the power to take her child away forever.

SOME DEALS NEVER STOPPED BEING ENFORCED.

The resolution of the fairy tale comes when the victim discovers the truth and calls out the abuser, which is exactly what happens during a successful T visa consultation. When the mother consults with an immigration attorney, we name the crime for what it is — severe human trafficking — and we explain the law, so she understands the employer does not actually have the legal power to steal her child.

By filing the T visa and potentially including her children as derivative beneficiaries, we hope to strip the trafficker of their leverage, keeping the family together and leaving the abuser completely powerless.

This story also indicates how some agreements or "deals" are unlawful or unenforceable. A survivor of trafficking may be coerced into appearing to have agreed to something, but such agreements would be void, voidable, or unenforceable by law. The force, fraud, or coercion removes the voluntariness from the deal, but the victim is made to feel they must comply.

The T Visa Policy Manual has a helpful section related to this, under the section on Peonage: "Peonage is a status or condition of involuntary servitude based upon real or alleged indebtedness. In other words, the perpetrator compels the victim into involuntary servitude in order to satisfy a real or artificially-created debt. When a debtor voluntarily enters into a contract to pay off a debt, that debtor, like any other contractor, can choose at any time to break the contract. It does not matter that a debtor entered into a contract agreeing to perform services or labor for the creditor. There is a clear distinction between peonage and voluntarily agreeing to perform labor or provide services in payment of a debt."

In the Rumpelstiltskin scenario, we may argue peonage related to the King's misconduct as well as involuntary servitude. Regarding Rumpelstiltskin, we may argue that when the Queen chose to break a contract, it does not negate the labor trafficking; and that even if there were an agreement, it was unlawful as obtained through coercion and void as a matter of public policy. In T screening training, pay attention to words like "agreed" and ask yourself if the person was coerced; if so, this is not a voluntary agreement (and therefore is not an agreement at all).

The "Pleasure Island" Trap: Pinocchio

The story of Pinocchio is usually remembered as a simple morality tale about a wooden puppet who needs to learn how to tell the truth. But if you look closely at the darkest chapter of his journey, you will find a depiction of international labor trafficking and fraudulent recruitment. Pinocchio and a group of runaway boys are lured onto a wagon heading to "Pleasure Island," a supposed paradise where there are no schools, no rules, and endless amusements. The recruiter uses fraud to transport these vulnerable minors, intentionally exploiting their youthful desire for an easy, glamorous life. An abuser can often easily see (or forces the victim to tell them) the personal, economic, sociocultural, and other factors that make the victim more vulnerable to being scared of this particular abuser and intentionally takes advantage of that to make the victim work or have sex.

Once the boys arrive and indulge in the island's treats, the trap door terrifyingly slams shut. The boys physically transform into donkeys, and the ruthless coachman who brought them there immediately sells them off to salt mines and circuses to perform grueling manual labor. The recruiter used deception to obtain them and transport them to a remote location, stripped them of their human autonomy, and subjected them to involuntary servitude. In the immigration context, we see this "Pleasure Island" dynamic when traffickers use exciting, too-good-to-be-true promises to recruit young people.

"Traffickers do not just sell fear; they frequently sell a glittering illusion that makes the victim entirely willing to walk right into the trap."

Let us look at how this plays out in a real-world consultation.

Imagine a sixteen-year-old boy named Marco living in Central America who loves playing sports. A well-dressed recruiter comes to his town claiming to represent an elite youth soccer academy in the United States. The recruiter tells Marco's family that if they pay a small initial fee, Marco will be transported to a prestigious training camp in Florida where he will attend a specialized sports school and eventually sign a highly paid professional contract. Marco is absolutely thrilled, willingly leaving his family behind while imagining a glamorous life of fame and athletic success.

When Marco arrives in Florida, the elite soccer academy turns out to be a complete illusion. Instead of a training camp, he is taken to an isolated agricultural facility where he is handed a machete and told he must work the fields from sunrise to sunset to pay off an exorbitant travel debt. When he cries and asks about playing soccer, the camp boss laughs and threatens to have him thrown into an adult immigration prison if he ever tries to run away.

When a client like Marco has escaped the situation and consults with you, he might feel intense shame for having believed the recruiter's extravagant lies. He might tell you that it was his own fault for being so foolish or naive about the sports academy, completely blaming himself for the situation. One of our team members who regularly screens potential clients for trafficking indicators told me that in such situations, clients often tend to minimize or self-blame, or avoid discussing certain topics, perhaps to feel better about themselves or to avoid being judged. So, additional or rephrased questions have proven useful, often at a later part of the screening session or on another day, when they feel more comfortable.

As Marco's attorney, you can gently help him understand that falling for a fraudulent promise does not negate the trafficking victimization in any way. The law specifically recognizes that fraud is a prohibited means of control, and you can use your T visa declaration to show the adjudicator exactly how the trafficker weaponized Marco's childhood dreams to force him into servitude.

When we file for a T visa and obtain a bonafide determination work permit or a full T visa approval with a T-status based work permit, one goal is to obtain work authorization for the client. Another is to make the client less susceptible to abuse if possible, as work authorization and protection from deportation could minimize future threats by others. It does not always work this way in practice, because threats can be terrifying even after the victim has escaped. But wherever we can work to disrupt an abuser's business model, we have an opportunity to help.

The "Sins of the Father" Trap: Rapunzel

The story of Rapunzel is memorable due to her long hair and the isolated tower, but the beginning of the story illustrates human trafficking. Before Rapunzel is born, her mother develops an intense, desperate craving for the radishes growing in the beautiful garden next door, which belongs to a powerful enchantress. The husband breaks into the garden to steal the radishes, but the enchantress catches him in the act and threatens him. To save himself, the husband agrees to a terrifying bargain: he can take all the radishes he wants, but he must surrender his unborn child to the enchantress as payment for his theft. When the baby is born, the enchantress immediately takes her away, names her Rapunzel, and eventually locks her in a secluded tower with no doors or stairs.

If we analyze this through the T visa framework, Rapunzel is a victim of severe human trafficking rooted in debt bondage. Her father incurred a debt to the enchantress by stealing the garden vegetables, and he literally pledged his child's life and freedom to satisfy that personal obligation. Rapunzel is then harbored in strict isolation, completely cut off from the outside world, and kept entirely under the control of the person holding the debt. The fact that she is a minor makes the situation even more legally straightforward, as the extreme power imbalance perfectly illustrates a condition of peonage and captivity. Under the T Visa Policy Manual, debt bondage is "the status or condition of a debtor arising from a pledge by the debtor of the personal services of the debtor or those of a person under the debtor's control as a security for debt, if the value of those services as reasonably assessed is not applied toward the liquidation of the debt or the length and nature of those services are not limited and defined." Rapunzel is never able to pay off the debt. She is also subjected to involuntary servitude.

In our law practice, we see this exact dynamic when massive smuggling debts are weaponized against vulnerable families. For example, a parent may incur a debt to a smuggler or an overseas loan shark to bring their family to the United States. When the parent cannot make the exorbitant weekly payments, the trafficker demands that the family's teenage daughter come work for them to pay off the balance.

The daughter is sent to work in a nail salon, a private home, or a convenience store, where her wages are entirely confiscated to pay for her father's "stolen radishes." She is kept isolated, threatened with harm to her family if she tries to escape, and trapped in a cycle of working off a debt that she never consented to in the first place.

According to the USCIS T Visa Policy Manual, involuntary servitude is induced by:

- "Means of any scheme, plan, or pattern intended to cause a person to believe that, if the person did not enter into or continue in such condition, that person or another person would suffer serious harm or physical restraint; or
- Abuse or threatened abuse of legal process."

Slavery "is generally understood to mean the state of being held under the complete and total ownership or control of another person or entity and being deprived of liberty, autonomy, and independence for the purpose of subjecting the victim to forced labor or services," (all definitions noted in the T Visa Policy Manual which you can access online: https://www.uscis.gov/policy-manual/volume-3-part-b).

We can use the definitions of involuntary servitude, debt bondage, peonage, and slavery, to analyze this hypothetical, and also note the overlap in concepts.

The "Family Duty" Trap: Cinderella

One common T visa case type we see is mirrored in the story of Cinderella. Most people focus entirely on the fairy godmother, the glass slipper, and the royal ball at the end of the tale. But if you read the first half of the story closely, it is a good study in domestic servitude, psychological coercion, and other T-Visa-level abuse by family members.

In the traditional story, after the young girl's mother dies and her father marries a new wife, the stepmother and stepsisters immediately strip her of her status and banish her to the kitchen. They force her to rise before daylight, carry water, make the fires, cook, and wash all the clothes, while constantly subjecting her to mockery and emotional abuse. She is denied a bed, forced to sleep in the dirt by the hearth, and completely isolated from the outside world. The stepmother uses her authority as the head of the household to extract endless, brutal, unpaid labor from a highly vulnerable dependent.

If we look at this narrative through the legal lens of the T visa, the stepmother is undeniably the trafficker. She is harboring the girl and using the means of psychological coercion, severe isolation, and the abuse of her familial relationship to subject the girl to involuntary servitude. The coercion here is particularly insidious because it is wrapped up in the complicated dynamics of a family unit. This makes it extremely difficult for the victim to recognize that she is actually being enslaved by the very people who are supposed to be providing her with care and shelter.

In our immigration practice, we see this exact "Cinderella" dynamic constantly, and it frequently involves labor trafficking disguised as benevolent family assistance. Imagine a seventeen-year-old girl whose parents in her home country can no longer afford to support her, so they arrange for her to travel to the United States to live with her aunt and uncle. The relatives promise her parents that they will enroll her in school and give her a wonderful life. But once she arrives, the aunt and uncle suddenly inform her that it cost them over $20,000 to bring her across the border, and that she must work for them to pay off this massive debt.

Instead of going to school, she is forced to clean their large house from top to bottom every single day, and then sent to work long, unpaid shifts at the family's restaurant. When she asks for money, asks to go to school, or complains about being exhausted, her relatives use intense cultural and familial coercion to silence her. They tell her that she is an ungrateful child, that she owes them for saving her from poverty, and that if she tries to leave, she will bring shame on her family. They effectively lock her in a condition of peonage, using the debt and their status as family elders as the ultimate mechanism of control.

When a client like this finally escapes and sits in your office for a consultation, she will often defend her abusers at first. She might look at you and say, "But my uncle helped me come to America, he is not a bad person," because she has been deeply conditioned to view her severe exploitation as a standard family obligation.

As her lawyer, you have to gently break through that psychological resistance and help her understand the objective facts of power and control. You have to teach her that family members absolutely can be traffickers, and that extracting forced, unpaid labor under the threat of deportation to pay off a smuggling debt constitutes severe human trafficking. Remember, traffickers use a "scheme, plan or pattern" and it's up to you, not your client, to recognize that objectively.

You may see an outwardly "happy" client.

In the Disney version of Cinderella, she's being labor trafficked, but she's also singing to birds and mice (the theme is resiliency in the face of exploitation by the very family whose love and protection she wants). Cinderella is a survivor who really just wants to be loved by her stepmother and stepsisters, one who suffered the loss of both biological parents.

Her ability to move through life may be true in part, but there is probably trauma lurking underneath. Therapy or other trafficking related support services may help both with her emotional needs and the strength of her legal case.

One thing about the Cinderella Story to keep in mind: In the old story book fairy tale, the Prince really is a hero. He figures out the shoe belongs to her and rescues her from her stepfamily. But is he a hero in the next book? Or does he "save" her only for himself? One thing we notice in T screening is sometimes a situation has been so bad at home that a vulnerable teenager is easily manipulated into leaving with a person who promises her something better, only to find out later, he's going to treat her like a servant too, or worse.

A colleague who has taught T visas for many years in CLE classes, once noted we may want to be on alert if Prince Charming appears while we have a pending T case, because that too can go from bad to worse. It is not uncommon for someone who has been trafficked, to be re-trafficked at a future time. Be wary of this while your T visa cases are pending.

In any event, Cinderella will forever be a famous story in the many versions we see — plays, books, cartoons, Netflix series. Ask yourself, in these many versions, where is the force, fraud or coercion? Are there multiple traffickers, like a family member, an employer, and an intimate partner? How does each situation make your client more vulnerable or more easily coerced by others?

THE "FAMILY DUTY" TRAP.
WHERE'S THE FORCE, FRAUD OR COERCION?

Consider the patterns you have observed in the fairy tails and how they align with this chart from the USCIS T Visa Policy Manual. The chart below breaks down the definition of a severe form of trafficking in persons into its three basic elements: action, purpose and means.

When you're looking at this chart, try to think of Cinderella stories that you know and where the action, purpose, and means appear in those narratives.

Severe Form of Trafficking in Persons Definition

Type of Trafficking	Action	Purpose	Means
Sex Trafficking	• Recruiting • Harboring • Transporting • Provision • Soliciting • Patronizing • Obtaining (Of a person)	For the purpose of a commercial sex act	Where the commercial sex act is induced by force, fraud, or coercion (Not required when the victim is under 18 years of age)
Labor Trafficking	• Recruiting • Harboring • Transporting • Provision • Obtaining (Of a person)	For the purpose of subjecting the victim to: • Involuntary servitude • Peonage • Debt bondage • Slavery	Through use of force, fraud, or coercion

Back to Reality: How Do I Screen?

Over the past decade, I have worked to standardize a trauma-informed screening method. While none are flawless, a systematic approach is vital. We should balance being thorough without compromising rapport or patience. Here are the foundational steps to effective screening:

1. Start by emphasizing confidentiality. Ensure the potential client is alone on the call and ask them to confirm no one else is listening, including their spouse. This is crucial, as potential clients may assume “no one” means anyone except their partner. Be clear about the confidentiality protections in place. Sample questions:

"Can you confirm that you're in a private and safe space right now?"

"Is there anyone who might be able to overhear this conversation?"

2. Review the intake form line by line with your potential client. Why? Because simple questions like "What is your real name and date of birth?" might lead to unexpected revelations, like, "I do not actually know." Many clients fill out intake forms only partially, or with the same biographic information they've always given but may actually not be what really happened in their life. By engaging with your standard intake form, you learn about their background, build trust, and gain insight into their experiences (and get ahead of any tricky bits to explain in the immigration filings). Sample questions:

"What would you like me to know about you that isn't on this form?"

"Could you tell me what happened the first time you were detained?"

3. Discuss their address, living situation, and whether they have a safe emergency contact. Explore their entry and exit history carefully, as this provides context. Sample questions:

"Is there someone you can trust who we can contact in an emergency?"

"Where did you stay right after being released from detention? Did you have a bed to sleep in?"

4. Address their workplace history, family dynamics, and relationships. Ask about children, significant others, marital history, parents, and siblings, as these elements are often interwoven with their experiences. Sample questions:

"What has been your experience with work here or in your home country?"

"Can you tell me about your parents? How has your relationship been with them?

What do you do at your current job?

Have police ever been to your house or did you ever have to call 911? Did anyone call the police for you, or did police ever show up without you realizing someone had called?

Were you ever married in the US? What about marrying in the church? Or did you marry before coming to the US? (sometimes they think marriage is only valid if done in the US, so we ask a few different ways; asking things a few different ways is the lynchpin of T visa screening)

Could you tell us a bit about your siblings? Are they in the U.S. like you, or do they live somewhere else?

What was the first kind of job you ever had, and how old were you? Can you tell me more?

Did you get to finish school? If not that's okay, but could we talk about why?

5. Allow space for clients to share more about their most difficult or exploitative experiences. For instance, inquire about their most challenging job or their harrowing experience entering the U.S. You can skip invasive questions initially and return to them after everyone feels more comfortable. Sample questions:

"What has been the most difficult job you've ever had?"

"What do you remember most about your journey to the U.S.?"

Did you ever get injured at work or see someone get really hurt?

Did you ever have problems with supervisors? What about stuff like discrimination at work?

Did someone ever sexually harass you? At work or online? For those who have experienced sexual harassment, this question may feel too invasive, so you may want to explain that term using examples of sexual harassment, such as *"has anyone ever touched you, even though you did not want it, or said something about the way you look that made you feel uncomfortable at work"* first. Others may need you to clearly say the words "sexual harassment" to understand what you are asking about.

6. If a person has never worked in the U.S., explore who financially supported them. Domestic household labor may not be recognized as work by clients, and it's essential to clarify this. If they indicate no religious affiliation or background, there's no need for extensive religious questions; instead, talk to them about what their home life looked like, and explore deeper if there's a history of domestic violence. Sample questions:

"Can you tell me more about how you managed financially while at home?"

"Have you felt pressure to fulfill roles in your home that felt unsafe?"

"Did someone ever tell you it's a [man's/woman's/girl's/boy's] job to do that kind of work?"

"Did you ever experience cultural or religious pressures that made you feel like you had to do something?"

7. The screening question list is not something that should be emailed for completion, typically. Screening usually requires a nuanced conversation between two humans, enhancing the potential for connection and understanding. It is worth taking the time to train yourself and your staff how to hold the space to have these patient, open, and trauma-informed conversations with your clients. If you email it to a client for them to complete, you may miss T cases.

8. Our screening encompasses various topics: smuggling turned trafficking, visa abuses, employment exploitation, religious coercion, and more. Our team of skilled professionals conduct these interviews, often requiring one to two hours to uncover significant details. Sample questions:

"Have you ever felt forced to take on jobs or responsibilities that made you feel unsafe?"

"Can you think of times when you felt you had no control over your work or living conditions?"

9. On a different occasion, the attorney will conduct a consultation, asking more focused legal questions based on detailed notes from the trauma-informed screening.

"What hopes or concerns do you have moving forward with your case?"

"Is there anything that you think I should keep in mind as we discuss your legal options?"

10. If our attorney identifies no immigration options, we engage in a roundtable discussion to ensure no trafficking indicators or other immigration paths were overlooked.

"Could we look up a bit more on the mushroom farming industry and see if there are OSHA violations or other questions we might have missed?"

"What about the prior spouse? I don't see that screening info here?"

11. Conclude the consultation as you began, reinforcing confidentiality and inviting the potential client to share anything they may have forgotten or any questions they may have. It's crucial to remember that trauma can impact memory; information may resurface later. Sample questions:

"Is there anything else you'd like me to know that you didn't feel able to share earlier?"

"Will you reach out to me if something comes to mind later?"

I often apologize for asking so many questions. If we have done our job well, the potential client might say "No, It helped." Or "No one has ever asked me this before." Still, I do not want clients to sign up for a case the same day. They should sleep on it, read a written legal fee agreement, and have a chance to go over it with our team again (in a language they understand) before retaining us. I want them to ask more questions, and bring up concerns or doubts they have, before retaining. It helps us avoid surprises and collaborate better together.

Final reminder on confidentiality and consultation style. If you allow both spouses, or the employer and employee, into the consultation because "they insist and the potential client is ok with it", what can happen?

Below is an example of a situation where the original individuals consulting may be traffickers, and the attorney may not be able to take the case for the victim, having met with the couple instead of with the victim. The attorney is now in a situation where she is facing issues about present danger to an individual, reporting versus confidentiality issues, and the potential criminal defense questions.

How would you find a T visa case if you let the nanny in the room with her potential sponsors, who may be trafficking her? A prepared immigration attorney would not do the consultation for the nanny, with her employers in the room. If you did that before and now want to rescreen someone you sent away, check with your state bar to be sure it is acceptable to screen for new information, if the childcare provider is willing to speak with you alone.

Another thing that can help your law practice is consistency. If you let people in the room just because they demand it, your paralegals and booking team don't have the tools they need to ensure consistency. If it's a standard rule applied to everyone, then it's easier to safely consult with potential clients. You're not doing anyone any favors by breaking your own rules.

Quiz: Force, Fraud, or Coercion

Let's check your new screening instincts before we move on. These questions are drawn from the patterns we've already discussed. No trick questions. Take a deep breath, count to four, and let it go slowly. No one is grading you. Also, the answer is right below the question..)

Question 1

Your potential client, Eloise, comes to you for a U visa consultation after being a victim of domestic violence. During your screening questions, she mentions that her employer — a family friend who sponsored her work visa — told her that the labor department is coming to inspect things since they were "dinged" for some "small wage violations." She is told she is going to get a check for some extra money, but she'll need to give it back in cash later because otherwise the company can't stay in business and immigration might come for workers like her. She continues working there despite not being paid her full wages and, out of fear, gives the employer the cash back. Which elements of trafficking are most clearly present in this scenario?

A) Force and Fraud

B) Fraud and Coercion

C) Only Fraud

D) None — this is a wage theft case, not trafficking

Answer: B — Fraud and Coercion.

Threatening to report someone to immigration authorities is a clear form of coercion. It doesn't require a fist or a locked door. The threat (direct or implied) itself is the mechanism of control, and it's powerful precisely because it exploits her immigration status. Fraud is also involved: they are falsely telling her that if she does not return part of the money in cash, ICE will somehow be more likely to arrest her. She keeps working — unpaid or underpaid — because she is scared others will be harmed or she might be arrested. Wage theft may also be present, making this one we might report to the U.S. DOL wage & hour crimes division as wage and hour violations that took place during the course of trafficking. The threat of harm (loss of liberty, freedom) used to maintain her labor is severe. This is the pattern that gets missed in consultations that stay too narrow. Once the coercion is identified, you can argue that any services performed were obtained through labor trafficking. One threat is enough to compel a person going forward.

Wait — but she came to you for a U visa for domestic violence! Not a T Visa based on employment. True. Maybe the domestic violence will be something for which you file a U visa. Also, you may screen her for coerced labor or sex that her abuser may have forced on her, and file for a T visa based on that. You may file the 'T' visa based on the labor trafficking at work and additional trafficking victimizations. What if she is only comfortable reporting one of the victimizations for a T visa? You may take a client-centered approach and assist with reporting the clearest victimization that your client is willing and able to report at this time.

Question 2

Your client, Amara, came to you initially asking about renewing her tourist visa. She wants you to file an I-539 B-1/B-2 extension of stay. The I-539 asks some questions like whether she has been employed at all, and if not, how will she support herself if the extension is granted. Through your screening questions, you learn the following: she has been living with a family for the past 4 months, caring for their three children. Her I-94 is expiring. She cleans the entire house daily, cooks all meals, and is on call from 5 a.m. until the children are in bed at night — sometimes past 11 p.m. Her "bedroom" is just the family's storage room with a cot tossed in. She has never been paid more than $50 a week. When she asked about payment, the family told her that her room and board covered her compensation and that if she left, they would not pay for her tourist visa extension. She does not have her passport — the family is "holding it for safekeeping." She loves the kids and doesn't want to see them hurt or neglected.

What form of trafficking is most clearly present here?

- A) Sex trafficking
- B) Slavery
- C) Involuntary servitude
- D) This is an employment dispute, not trafficking

Answer: C — Involuntary Servitude.

Amara did not come to you saying she was trafficked. She came to you about a visa renewal, and you already know she isn't eligible for extending her visa due to unauthorized work and status violations. That is exactly how these cases walk through the door. You can't (and won't) lie on the I-539 about unauthorized work. You instead may advise her about a T visa option.

Involuntary servitude exists when someone is compelled to work through force, fraud or coercion (or, the trafficker uses a scheme, pattern or plan with that goal). Amara is not choosing to stay because the arrangement suits her. She is staying because the family holds her passport, because the shame or fear of visa cancellation has been dangled as a consequence of leaving, and because she has nowhere to go.

The job duties themselves tell a story too. This is not a nanny who watches the kids from nine to five. This is a person performing the full domestic labor of a household — cooking, cleaning, childcare, all day, every day — subjected to wage and hour violations, isolation, and exhaustion. The room and board framing is a manipulation. It repackages exploitation as generosity.

The passport retention alone should stop you in your tracks and make you look closer with your T visa glasses. That detail is not incidental. It is a control mechanism. It signals that someone in that house knows exactly what they are doing to Amara.

When you hear about a storage room, no passport, low pay, and a looming visa extension cancellation, you are not looking at an employment dispute. You are looking at a T visa case.

The family holding Amara's visa extension over her head is not just cruel. It is legally significant in a way that changes the entire character of her situation.

When the family told Amara that her room and board was her compensation, and that they would withdraw their help with her visa extension if she didn't comply and keep working — they invoked the immigration system as a weapon. They used the threat of a legal process, specifically the extension application, to coerce her continued labor. That is textbook abuse of the legal process, and it satisfies one of the three regulatory definitions of coercion under the T visa framework.

The USCIS Policy Manual defines coercion to include three things. Let me quote it directly so you have it in front of you:

Threats of serious harm to or physical restraint against any person; any scheme, plan, or pattern intended to cause a person to believe that failure to perform an act would result in serious harm to or physical restraint against any person; or abuse or threatened abuse of the legal process.

The regulation at 8 C.F.R. § 214.201 defines that last prong precisely:

Abuse or threatened abuse of the legal process means the use or threatened use of a law or legal process whether administrative, civil, or criminal, in any manner or for any purpose for which the law was not designed, in order to exert pressure on another person to cause that person to take some action or refrain from taking some action.

The visa extension process exists to allow people to lawfully extend temporary status. It was not designed to be dangled over a domestic worker's head to guarantee her compliance. The moment this family leveraged that process to control Amara's behavior, they crossed into coercion under the statute.

Once coercion is established, every hour of labor Amara performed from that point forward is involuntary servitude under federal law. Every meal she cooked. Every child she bathed at ten o'clock at night. Every floor she scrubbed. Even if she loves those kids — and I believe her when she says she does — her emotional bond to them does not retroactively make her labor voluntary. Coercion poisons consent. That is the point of the definition.

Before we move into Chapter Three, I want you to pause here.

Think back over your visa overstay consultations. Any of them. The B-1/B-2 tourist who never left. The H-4 dependent whose spouse's petition fell apart. The H-2 seasonal worker who missed the departure window. The J-1 exchange visitor who stayed after the program ended. The K-1 fiancé(e) whose relationship dissolved. The H-1B whose employer withdrew the petition without warning.

Did any of those consultations have details that are sitting differently with you now? Write them down here — just enough to jog your memory later. No names, no identifying information. Just the pattern. The fact that caught your eye. The detail you filed away and moved on from.

Details from past consultations that might have been trafficking indicators:

1.

2.

3.

4.

Visa overstay consultation patterns I want to revisit:

3

How Trafficking Appears in Consults (The Hypos)

Note: As with other scenarios in this book, this chapter relies on hypotheticals so practitioners can see the law in action. I have found that people learn best from hearing about examples of trafficking. We're going to talk about a few hypos, but keep in mind that there are thousands of potential scenarios and none of the hypos here are based on any specific person or event.

Hypothetical: A client comes in asking about a marriage-based green card. Before we even begin discussing the details of his case, he tells me he does not want to be screened for a victim visa. That is understandable, so instead of pushing back, I take his lead and walk through the marriage-based path first. I am taking his goals seriously and will work through employment-based and marriage-based analyses first (not because they are better, but because considering all options is important).

As we work through his immigration history, the inadmissibility issues start stacking up. Multiple entries without inspection. Significant unlawful presence. Also, he recently has used the identity of a U.S. citizen to work. At that point, the marriage-based sponsorship strategy is no longer viable because certain immigration bars simply cannot be waived in the context of a marriage-based sponsorship. We walk through that together discussing how the application forms require disclosure of the grounds of inadmissibility he has triggered, and which grounds are unwaivable for a family-based or employment-based case. Once we shift the conversation, I ask about his work history. He has spent years in roofing. If you practice in this area, you already know what that tends to mean: no harness, dangerous heights, injuries that go unreported, paychecks that arrive late or not at all, and a steady stream of threats — sometimes subtle, sometimes not — tied to immigration status. At first, he describes the job the way many immigrant workers do: carefully, with a kind of practiced neutrality. But as we talk through the details, the story starts to change.

Several years earlier he had seriously injured his hand on the job. His supervisor told him he would not qualify for workers' compensation because he was "illegal," and that he needed to get back to work or his medical bills would never be paid. He believed it. He went back to work while still injured.

That single detail — the deliberate lie about workers' compensation eligibility, used to manipulate an injured worker to work before healing — is a trafficker's coercion tactic. By the end of the consultation, we have a completely different legal strategy. Not a marriage case. A T visa case which has the added benefit of an expanded waiver of the inadmissibility issues he would otherwise face.

Construction & Roofing Exploitation T Visas

Let's explore a hypothetical with fact patterns involving dangerous working conditions, workers misclassified as independent contractors, lies about workers' compensation eligibility, and coercion based on workplace injuries.

A man calls for a consultation about getting a work permit. He's been in the U.S. for twelve years, undocumented, and he works in roofing. His employer classifies him as an independent contractor. He gets paid cash. No benefits, no workers' comp, no paid overtime.

Halfway through the consultation, when asked about whether he has ever been hurt on the job, he mentions he fell off a roof two years ago. Broke his wrist. His boss told him that because he was a contractor, he couldn't file a workers' compensation claim because he was illegal and because it would get the company shut down. So, he went back to work. Wrist still not right. Never saw a doctor. The boss kept saying he'd have to work through the pain to pay the bills.

That's not an employment classification problem. It is fraud and coercion used to compel continued labor — i.e. the implied threat of immigration reporting as leverage to keep a worker on the job after an injury is textbook trafficking.

That's the case you almost miss. Ask if they have been injured. If they say no, ask again gently, like "Wow, you have been working 12 years in a hard, dangerous roofing career? In all those years, nothing ever happened?"

You might get a laugh or a moment of hesitation, then more information. When you're hired on the T visa case, you're requesting his medical records and photos of the permanent scars on his wrist from a fall he might not have disclosed if you had not taken some time to be practical about industry day-to-day experiences.

Also, be understanding that it's okay to have feelings that are mixed. A person may have been legally victimized but still not want to cause others harm, and they may have learned a lot of industry-specific skills at a job where they were trafficked. Or they may be reflecting on the good days at that job, not on their present injuries or harm they suffered in the past, in the moment you are interviewing them.

Survivors of labor trafficking might compartmentalize profound physical harm. They may also simply not realize you meant you actually wanted details of injuries they consider to be common, or they may be thinking of injuries others had that were worse than their own industry-specific ones. They may have started the consultation process thinking the case would only involve them, so talking about other people in their lives (or complaining about them) may feel uncomfortable.

Roofing Case Questions

The questions I ask in a roofing case aren't generic. They're built for the industry.

1. Who bought your tools and equipment, and did you ever have to pay your boss back for them?

2. Did your boss control which job sites you went to,

or could you choose your own work? Remember, independent contractors are supposed to control their fees, tools, hours, and safety arrangements. When the "boss" prevents that, the independence goes away and you have an involuntary employment arrangement.

3. Were you ever told you owed money for transportation to job sites, or for motels he arranged for roofing jobs out of town? Were there times he took you to a site and you weren't able to leave as planned?

4. If you said you were too sick or hurt to work, what happened? Did he ever show up at your house, send others to get you, or blow up your phone with calls and texts?

5. Did your boss ever drive you somewhere after he'd been drinking, or demand you drive others without a license?

6. Were you ever asked to work on a roof without fall protection equipment? When you brought it up, what did he say?

7. Cuss words. I've heard them all. What language is used on the job site? What's the worst thing you ever heard him call you or someone else? It is awkward, but sometimes I will directly ask if they used the word "mother-f#$%^" when I can tell they don't want to offend me or seem disrespectful. There's so much respect that goes to me in a consult, and I want to give them permission to tell me the nasty stuff that was really said aloud. I believe sometimes attorneys are in so many adversarial situations as part of their work, that we may minimize or forget that potential clients

respect us too much to say cuss words, even if they are describing labor abuses. If they do disclose the abusive language to you, acknowledge your appreciation of their honesty, and as one trafficking investigator told me, let them know it paints a clearer picture of what happened, as well as possibly strengthening their case.

8. Guns. Did your boss bring guns or knives or other weapons to work? What was the excuse for that?

9. How old is your boss? Is he bigger than you? Does he flash money and cars and vacations for himself but then not have payroll for you come Friday? Did your boss ever make abusive comments to your co-workers? Threats to others may demonstrate what harm the trafficker would inflict on both the co-workers and your client, if anyone were to disobey. Flashing money and making false promises to pay and acting larger than life, contribute to a coercive environment and may constitute fraud. Use of physical size or nationality as privilege to intimidate workers, is another power-and-control mechanism.

10. Did he promise you more work if you got this job done, although he still hasn't paid you for the last one? Did checks ever bounce? Or did he tell you that you have to wait to cash them? Did he ever refuse to give you a 1099 or W-2?

It's so many questions! We could talk about one job for an hour. But when you listen to the answers your client gives, you'll find your foray into human resources, job duties, contractor rules, and the construction industry was worth it.

Gas Stations, Convenience Stores, Franchise Food, and Motels

These scenarios — often involving workers recruited from South Asia, and often featuring unpaid "training" periods, extremely long shifts, employer-provided housing, verbal humiliation, and forced exposure to dangerous situations like armed robberies — give rise to T visa eligibility.

Certain industries are notorious for exploiting undocumented workers, and the abuses often cross the legal threshold into human trafficking. For example, we regularly see cases involving individuals from India or other countries who are recruited to work in gas stations, convenience stores, food franchises, or motels. The employer promises good pay and a path to a visa, or even eventual store ownership or partnerships, but upon arrival, the reality is a nightmare. The victim is made to work excessive hours, sleep on the premises in deplorable conditions, and endure verbal humiliation or threats of deportation. The employer might even lie and claim that the initial training period must be unpaid, effectively stealing months of labor while isolating the worker from the outside world. Sweat equity scams with false promises to pay or to allow partnership are common in these industries where people start as cashiers with the goal of eventual chain/franchise ownership.

Let me walk you through a hypothetical that looks, on the surface, like a wage theft consultation.

Motel hypo: A woman from India contacts us about a U visa certification for a home invasion which local police would not sign. Her English is limited, so we use a Gujarati interpreter from the start. At first, she says she never worked. Then she said she did but has no proof of it and it was only 3 weeks. She worked at a motel for three weeks, left after what she describes as a scary work environment, and her final week's pay was never sent to her. Also, for the first week she was told it would be unpaid training. Also, these are distant family, so it is only with much reassurance of confidentiality that we find out anything at all.

Standard wage claim, right?

I start with my open-ended questions. *Where did she sleep?* On the property. *Who arranged that?* The owner. *Did she pay rent?* No, but it came out of her wages. *How many hours a day did she work?* She pauses. Fifteen, sometimes more.

Who else worked there?

Just her and the owner's family.

Did she ever leave the property?

Rarely.

Did the owner ever cross the line, or touch you without permission?

Yes. He called her names and once grabbed her hand inappropriately.

Did he ever do something harmful again?

Another time, he forced a kiss on her and then made an excuse.

Did she tell anyone?

No. This is the first time she has ever told someone. She felt if she said anything it would destroy her family and she would be punished. She believed that because the owner said not to tell anyone and to just do her job if she wanted to have a place to stay.

How did she leave?

Finally, she called an uncle who picked her up and took her to live with him. She did not tell the uncle what happened.

There it is.

Three weeks feels short, but trafficking for a T visa has **no minimum duration requirement**. In this scenario, she is subjected to false promises to pay wages (fraud); she is coerced via isolation, physical/sexual force, and threat of homelessness or banishment if she did not perform services.

I want to flag something important here, because this comes up when attorneys first encounter "short-duration" cases.

The USCIS Policy Manual speaks directly to this. Under the section on No Defined Length of Time Required, it states:

> "To establish that they are or have been a victim of trafficking and have been compelled to perform the labor or services, applicants do not need to show that they were victimized for a defined length of time. For example, in the context of involuntary servitude, the duration of time can be of varying length and may be short in duration."

The Policy Manual confirms that labor doesn't have to be coerced every single moment. There can be voluntary periods mixed with involuntary ones. What matters is that at least some portion of the work was involuntary.

What you're actually evaluating is whether the totality of circumstances shows the trafficker's purpose was to create a condition of servitude. Three weeks of isolation, unpaid "training," sexual assault used as a control mechanism, and threats of homelessness go far beyond a wage theft case. This is the calculated methodology (i.e., "scheme, pattern or plan") of a trafficker.

Duration is only one data point, and the trafficker's "scheme, pattern or plan" can be just as relevant.

Landscaping and Outdoor Labor

Scenarios covering H-2B temporary worker visa abuses, as well as abuses of undocumented workers — crew isolation, transportation control, pesticide exposure, and the "hook and reel" wage tactic are all flags to consider for a T visa case.

We see similar patterns in outdoor labor industries like landscaping and construction. Workers might be hired informally or even brought in on H-2B visas, only to find their passports confiscated and their movements heavily monitored. In outdoor labor roles, workers are frequently denied basic OSHA safety equipment like gloves, safety glasses, appropriate footwear, and helmets.

Also, some landscapers never came to the U.S. on a visa — they came here without papers. When a worker inevitably gets injured, such as severely cutting their hand, the employer might lie and say undocumented immigrants do not qualify for workers' compensation or will be deported if they go to the hospital for help. This abuse of the legal process forces the employee to work through immense pain to pay off their debts, cementing the coercive environment.

When dealing with cases like these, practitioners often get tripped up on the physical presence requirement. A very common mistake is thinking that to win a T visa, the trafficker must have been the one who brought the victim into the United States. That is simply not true. The law requires that the applicant be physically present in the United States on account of the trafficking. This means showing how the past trauma impacts their daily life and current presence, such as receiving necessary physical therapy for that injured hand or undergoing mental health counseling that is not reasonably available in their home country. By connecting your clients to the help they need, you are not only building a stronger legal case, but you are actively aiding in their recovery and survival.

When I'm preparing to consult with someone who may have experienced labor trafficking in landscaping, agriculture, or outdoor construction, my goal is to ask questions that invite disclosure rather than provoke defensiveness or silence. We don't interrogate, we ask open ended questions, listen carefully, and ask respectful follow up questions.

Landscaping and Outdoor Labor Questions

Here are some questions I return to again and again in these consultations:

1. **"How did you first hear about this job, and who told you about it?"** Recruitment fraud starts somewhere. I want to know if a recruiter, a friend, a family member, or a labor broker made promises that turned out to be false.

2. **"Before you started working, what were you told you would earn, and what did you actually receive?"** The gap between those two numbers tells me everything about the "hook."

3. **"Did anyone hold onto your passport, ID, or any of your documents at any point?"** Document confiscation is a red flag — it implies taking away

freedom to move or leave.

4. **"Were you able to come and go freely, or did someone control how you got to and from work?"** Transportation control is coercion. I need to know whether they had any independent mobility.

5. **"Were you ever told you owed money for your housing, your transportation, your tools, or your visa fees — money that was being taken out of your pay?"** Debt bondage hides in paycheck deductions that never seem to shrink.

6. **"Did you ever work without being paid, and were you told it was for training or to pay something off?"** There is a myth that training should be unpaid labor. This flags for fraud as well as abuse of the legal process (coercion) to obtain unpaid labor.

7. **"Were you ever exposed to chemicals, pesticides, or other hazards without being given protective equipment or being told what you were working with?"** Pesticide exposure without disclosure or protection is both a labor violation and a coercion tool.

8. **"If you were hurt at work, what happened? Did anyone help you get medical care?"** Injury responses reveal whether the employer treated this person as a human being or a liability.

9. **"Were you ever threatened — with deportation, with not being paid, with being fired or reported — when you complained or tried to leave?"** In these scenarios, it doesn't have to be a direct threat. Sometimes it is a joke about ICE, sometimes it is commenting frequently about immigration status,

sometimes it is an employer acting like they are protecting them while making them feel ingratiated as well as afraid the employer might turn on them if they don't obey.

10. **"Is there anyone you felt you couldn't talk to, or anywhere you felt you couldn't go, while you were working for this employer?"** Isolation is coercion. Sometimes clients don't name it that way, but they feel it.

Smuggling Turned Trafficking (STT) / "Stash House" Traps

Situations where a voluntary smuggling agreement turns into forced labor, such as victims being locked in stash houses and forced to cook and clean for other migrants, or cases where migrants are forced to work in Mexico before crossing and are unfree to leave through arrival in the U.S. (or in some cases, slightly before entry).

The "Stash House" Trap: When the Trip Becomes a Job

Let's look at a scenario that happens far more often than many immigration lawyers realize. Imagine a person named Jay who wants to get to the United States to find work. His parents in India are drowning in debt, and the family feels enormous pressure to change their financial situation. They find a smuggler who promises a quick, safe, and worry-free trip to the United States for an agreed-upon fee.

The agent also claims that Jay will have legitimate visas to get close to the U.S. border, which supposedly makes the journey safer, but also much more expensive. On its face, this sounds like a standard smuggling deal where Jay is technically a willing participant in crossing without papers. But once the journey begins, the situation changes drastically.

Jay is taken to a stash house near the border where he is locked inside and told he cannot leave until his family pays more money. While trapped in the house, the smugglers force him to cook meals for the other migrants, clean the bathrooms, and perform daily chores to earn his meager food and water. He is threatened with violence and warned that if he tries to run, he will be killed or reported to immigration. Trafficking does not always begin in a workplace or inside a home. Sometimes it begins on the road to the United States, in a locked stash house, where a promise of transportation suddenly becomes a demand for labor.

Before the T Visa Policy Manual was published in 2021 and before the regulatory updates that followed, adjudicators were often dismissive of these scenarios. They frequently labeled them as mere exploitation or treated them as nothing more than a smuggling crime that had gotten out of hand. Because of that environment, many of these cases required appeals and federal litigation. In several situations, we ended up filing lawsuits challenging the denial of the T visa petitions.

In *L.A.A.M. v. Zuchowski*, Case No. 5:22-cv-173 (D. Vt. Sept. 27, 2024), the court confirmed that a person who escaped from a stash house where he was held under guard and forced to perform labor was a victim of trafficking. The court emphasized that the regulations do not require trafficking to last for a specific minimum period of time. Even relatively short periods of compelled labor can satisfy the definition of involuntary servitude. While it is sometimes seemingly easier to use subsequent trafficking events as the foundation of the T visa case, do not underestimate the viability of smuggling-turned-trafficking claims.

In my professional experience over many years, as confirmed by FBI law enforcement agents I have reported to or spoken with, sex trafficking for women frequently occurs in smuggling-turned-trafficking cases. We also see this more commonly in cases for transgender clients, and overall, there appears to be more targeting of individuals who traffickers on the border or in stash-houses seem to think present as LGBTQ+. Regardless of identity or orientation, sex trafficking victimizations are extremely painful, and people may avoid talking about them for a long time. This is understandable — for a potential client to hope they can complete their case based on truthful labor trafficking without having to go into sex trafficking details. We can simply be mindful, compassionate, and remember that clients may open up over time if they feel more comfortable and trust us to be respectful and helpful. The "Why didn't you tell me this before?" comments would be inappropriate, knowing the level of trauma traffickers impose and how hard it is for anyone to come forward.

Practitioner Alert: Recently there have been accounts from lawyers that USCIS is issuing Requests for Evidence on T visa cases solely based on "smuggling turned trafficking" and claiming that the applicant may be inadmissible because of "material assistance of terrorism." (the "TRIG" bar). This is frustrating because not only does the Policy Manual explicitly mention smuggling turned trafficking as an independent basis of eligibility, but also there is clear duress involved that makes any "assistance" a tool of the trafficker, not intentional cooperation in a smuggling/trafficking ring. Additionally, from a law enforcement perspective, it would not make sense for Congress to create a T visa category to help law enforcement prosecute the most dangerous cartels for trafficking, while simultaneously making it so victims of those organizations are deemed inadmissible for acts they did not willfully commit. Proceed with caution and screen for another trafficking incident that could be a more favorable basis for the T. Prepare yourself and the client for the possibility of a TRIG RFE or the need to appeal a denial related to grounds of inadmissibility. Keep in touch with other practitioners nationwide to learn about any successful rebuttals to this seeming attempt to cut out a valid basis of eligibility. As trends do, they often go away, so this is also a practitioner alert for advocacy related to unjust TRIG-bar accusations, and for lawyers preparing victim statements to be careful to avoid over-generalizing information.

Quiz: Stash House Scenarios

Before we move on, let's make sure this framework is locked in. Here is a quiz question!

Question: Jay was smuggled into the United States under a paid agreement with a smuggling network. While held in a stash house near the border, he was forced to cook and clean for other migrants under threat of violence. Jay's family eventually paid the additional money demanded. He was released after they transported him into Texas, but not before he was made to cook and clean for 2 more days. Jay is now living in the United States and receiving mental health counseling.

Which of the following is true?

A) Jay cannot qualify for a T visa because he voluntarily agreed to be smuggled.

B) Jay cannot qualify for a T visa because his trafficker did not bring him to the United States for the purpose of trafficking.

C) Jay may qualify for a T visa because the smuggling agreement transformed into forced labor through threats and coercion.

D) Jay cannot qualify for a T visa because his trafficking situation lasted only a short period of time.

Answer: The answer is C. Jay may qualify for a T visa because the smuggling agreement transformed into forced labor through threats and coercion.

A voluntary smuggling arrangement does not disqualify someone from T visa protection when the circumstances shift into force, fraud, or coercion. Neither duration nor original voluntary intent determines eligibility. The T Visa Policy Manual states, "A consensual smuggling agreement does not excuse any acts of trafficking that may arise during the course of smuggling. However, as with all cases, the applicant must establish the perpetrator's purpose. In cases involving smuggling, this may include establishing that the smuggler's motivation or purpose shifted over time to that of a trafficker and that the initial consent has been invalidated by the actions of the smuggler-turned-trafficker."

Domestic Violence-Based Trafficking (DV-T) and the "Cinderella" Trap

Cases where intimate partner violence is specifically used as a mechanism to force domestic labor or sex acts, as well as situations involving debt bondage and peonage disguised as family assistance (such as abuse from in-laws) can qualify a domestic violence victim for a T Visa.

A client came in describing what sounded, at first, like a domestic violence case. In one sense it was — the physical abuse was real, and it was serious. But as the consultation continued, the picture grew larger.

Her partner had controlled where she lived, where she worked, and who she was allowed to speak to. When she had tried to leave, he threatened her with immigration consequences. There had been moments — more than a few — where she was pressured into work situations she did not feel free to refuse. Once, when a neighbor called 911 because they heard yelling from her house, she told the responding officers that nothing had happened, too scared to tell the truth.

In a domestic violence case, that recantation might raise complications. In a T visa consultation, it is something I note and move past. I am not building a criminal prosecution. I am trying to understand what actually happened, and what the path forward looks like — including, if the client chooses, a report to law enforcement at a time and in a manner she controls.

The coercive control details did not come out all at once. They emerged slowly, the way they usually do. She had framed her experience almost entirely in terms of the physical abuse, which is what she expected a lawyer to care about. The broader pattern only became visible when we talked through the full shape of her daily life during that period — who made decisions, who held money, what she had to do around the house, what happened when she tried to say no.

By the end of the consultation, it was clear this was not only a domestic violence case. It was a DV-T — a T visa case in which intimate partner violence was the mechanism of coercion. The legal strategy looked very different from what either of us had expected when we started.

When Domestic Violence Is Actually Human Trafficking

As immigration lawyers, we see domestic violence and intimate partner cases all the time. It is easy to put on our U visa or VAWA glasses and stop analyzing once we hear about physical abuse or a police report. I have seen many cases where a person consults with us saying that every lawyer they spoke with told them there was nothing they could do because the person didn't cooperate with law enforcement in the past, or the divorce happened too long ago to help.

Then we start asking more questions, and suddenly the case looks completely different. We find out the abuser controlled all the money, forced the victim to work in a family business without pay, or used threats of deportation to keep the victim in a condition of servitude. Sometimes the abuser brings the victim into the country on a fiancé visa or spousal petition, only to lock them in the house and treat them like an unpaid maid. This is something we call a DV-T, which is shorthand for a trafficking case where domestic or intimate partner violence becomes the coercion that results in involuntary servitude or sex trafficking.

> A person's life and safety are "a thing of value."

It is also vital to understand that commercial sex trafficking does not just mean forced prostitution. According to the law, a commercial sex act means any sex act on account of which anything of value is given to or received by any person. A person's life, their physical safety, or their ability to see their children again are all things of value. If an abuser forces a victim to perform sex acts in exchange for not being beaten or killed, that meets the definition of commercial sex trafficking. Lawyers frequently miss this because they assume sex trafficking requires the exchange of cash or involves strangers.

Quiz: A Thing of Value and the T visa

Rosa was brought to the United States by her boyfriend on a tourist visa. He housed her, fed her, and controlled every dollar she spent. When she refused to clean the house or cook for his extended family, he beat her. When she refused sex, he beat her harder and reminded her that without him, she would be deported and never see her daughter again. She had no money, no phone, no way out.

Question: What claims may Rosa have under the T visa framework?

Answer: The answer is both sex and labor trafficking.

Rosa's forced domestic labor — cooking, cleaning, and serving the household — under threat of violence constitutes involuntary servitude. The coercion is the beating and the threat of deportation. The thing extracted is her labor.

Rosa's forced sex acts also meet the definition of commercial sex trafficking, even though no money changed hands. Her safety, her ability to remain in the country, and her access to her daughter are all things of value. Her boyfriend received something of value every time he coerced her — her compliance, her body, her silence.

One victim. One abuser. Two forms of severe trafficking. This is exactly the kind of case that disappears into the domestic violence file and never gets the relief it deserves unless you have your T visa glasses on.

> **Pro Tip:** Words matter in victim statements. You need to describe commercial sex trafficking. If you use criminal legal terms like "rape" or "molestation" instead, you may confuse the USCIS officer, causing them to miss the trafficking elements. It's fine for clients to use those words, naturally and rightfully, to describe their experience, but the T visa statement should be focused on the actions that meet the statutory elements of a commercial sex act. Your job is to validate their lived experience while legally translating those facts to show how they meet the definition of commercial sex trafficking. We do not want a denial of a T visa case due to terminology errors, when there are multiple crimes that took place, and where the only one that can result in a T visa approval is trafficking. For example, "he raped me in exchange for my life" may be better described in a statement as "he forced a sex act on me in exchange for my life."

Restaurants and Hotels

Cases involving wage theft, excessive hours, the "work ethic" trap, tip manipulation, employer housing control, abuse of cleaning crew team members, sexual harassment and more.

Hypo: The Hotel/Motel Cleaner

Fatima came to the U.S. on a work visa and took a housekeeping job at a mid-size hotel. Her supervisor told her that if she worked hard and cleaned extra rooms, she'd be promoted to lead housekeeper within six months. That promotion never came. Instead, she was assigned the workload of two employees after a co-worker quit and was never replaced. Her paychecks arrived weeks late, and when she asked about it, her supervisor called her stupid and lazy in front of the other staff. She developed chemical burns on her hands from bleach-based cleaners she was given no gloves to handle. When she finally quit, she came to you for help.

Question: Does Fatima have a potential T visa claim based on involuntary servitude?

A) No, because she ultimately left voluntarily.

B) No, because there were no physical restraints or threats of deportation.

C) Yes, because the combination of false promises, wage manipulation, unsafe conditions, and psychological abuse may constitute involuntary servitude even without physical confinement.

D) Yes, but only if she filed a wage complaint before leaving.

Answer: The answer is C.

Let me walk you through why.

A is wrong because voluntary departure doesn't erase what happened before it. The fact that Fatima eventually found a way out doesn't mean the conditions that trapped her weren't coercive.

B is wrong because involuntary servitude doesn't require chains or an ICE threat whispered in someone's ear. Psychological coercion, financial manipulation, and abuse that make a reasonable person feel they cannot leave are enough. Fatima's supervisor created an environment of humiliation and dependence to coerce her. A law enforcement officer without specialized trafficking training might gravitate toward answer B. They may ask, 'But were you physically free to leave?' in a manner that pressures a traumatized victim into saying 'yes,' prematurely concluding it isn't trafficking. They are incorrect.

D is wrong because there is no administrative pre-filing requirement for a T visa. We are not penalizing survivors for failing to navigate bureaucratic systems while they were being exploited. As the T visa lawyer, you can help her report her victimization.

C is correct because the statute looks at the totality of the circumstances. False promises got Fatima in the door. Wage manipulation kept her financially destabilized. Unsafe conditions damaged her health. Psychological abuse eroded her confidence. Each element alone might look like a bad job. Together, they build a coercion picture worth examining carefully.

Restaurants and Food Service Questions

Here are ten questions I ask in restaurant and food service consultations:

1. How did you find out about this job, and what were you told before you started?

2. How many hours do you work each week, and how are you paid? Walk me through a day from the time you would wake up until going to sleep.

3. Have you ever worked through an injury or illness because you felt you had no choice? Did your hand get cut at work? Did you ever slip on the floor?

4. Did your employer control where you live or how you get to work?

5. Has anyone ever threatened you, insulted you, or humiliated you at work?

6. Are there deductions taken from your pay that you didn't agree to? Did your employer keep a "semana de fondo" ("week's fund"), like an anti-leaving deposit, when you started the job?

7. What happens when you complain about your conditions?

8. Has your employer ever commented on your sexuality, immigration status, or family situation in a way that felt like a warning?

9. Do you feel free to quit this job if you wanted to?

10. Is there anything about your work situation you've never told anyone?

Restaurant Hypo: Let's imagine my paralegal flagged this consultation before it landed on my desk. The potential client, I'll call him Daniel, had called twice asking for a guarantee that we'd take his case before he'd agree to pay the consultation fee.

My staff is trained for this. We cannot evaluate a case we haven't heard. We cannot promise an outcome, we cannot guarantee results, and we certainly can't guess if someone even has a case at all, without a comprehensive consultation. That's not how ethical legal practice works. They explain that clearly, with patience, and Daniel books a consultation.

When I get on the call with Daniel, the first thing he tells me is that his boss is a great man. Taught him everything about running a kitchen. Daniel has real pride in his voice when he says it.

Then, in the same breath, he tells me he works seventy hours a week.

"And overtime?" I ask.

He pauses. "He says salaried people don't get overtime."

Daniel is not salaried. He has no written contract. He gets a flat weekly amount regardless of whether he works forty hours or seventy. His boss simply decided the word "salary" covered whatever arrangement he invented.

The kitchen has no functioning HVAC. Summer in a professional kitchen without ventilation isn't uncomfortable — it's dangerous. Daniel tells me the fans broke in August, and the boss never fixed it. The summer was brutal.

Last February, Daniel got the flu. Fever, body aches, the kind of sickness where you can barely stand. His boss called him personally... but not to wish him well.

"He said if I didn't come in, he'd find someone who wanted the job."

Daniel cooked for a full dining room with a fever over a hundred degrees.

When Daniel finally voices any complaint — about the heat, about the hours, about anything — his boss has a response ready.

"He calls me gay." Daniel says it quietly, like he's still deciding whether it matters. "If I say something hurts or I'm tired, he says I'm being gay about it. He does it to customers too, behind their backs. Makes jokes." He stops. "But he taught me so much."

The humiliation is consistent. Targeted. It functions as a silencer.

This is a T visa case. The difference now is that I have trained screeners, so they will go through many questions before I ever have the consultation. By the time I have the consultation, I may have follow up questions, or maybe Daniel will reveal more, but most of our consultation will likely focus on the legal steps. Like would he be willing to allow us to make a report to the Dept. of Labor? Could we connect him to Trafficking Victim Assistance Program (TVAP) services and therapy?

Then we walk through the benefits of the T visa. Daniel may not start a case with us immediately. He's been in the job a long time, and he just wants the bad parts to stop. He doesn't want to get anyone in trouble. So, we will likely have a follow up call the next time Daniel's boss blows up at him, and Daniel will know we will be ready when he is ready.

Acknowledge the Learning Curve

You will miss cases. I have missed cases. I am sure there are people who have been trafficked but still do not feel comfortable coming forward. Some people aren't going to be ready to tell you their life story, and others will be too afraid to file the T visa case. The goal is a commitment to keep looking, keep learning, build trust genuinely, and keep asking questions when something doesn't sit right.

Chapter 4 is where we get into what happens after you identify the case. You've done the screening. You see the indicators. Now what? Now we build it. We talk about declarations, law enforcement certification, supporting evidence, and how to prepare your client for what comes next.

4

T Visa Evidence: Prosecution Not Required

The Myth of the Police Incident Report

Every few weeks in our training sessions, I watch the energy shift. An attorney shows up having done everything right — careful screening, trauma-informed interviewing, a client who trusts them, a fact pattern that checks every box. They're excited. But, they may have issues they are worried about, like:

"My client never reported it to the police."

"The trafficker died two years ago."

"The business shut down."

"Our county sheriff has made it very clear he doesn't consider undocumented people crime victims."

"Law enforcement took the report and closed it as unsubstantiated. Said it wasn't trafficking."

"Police said we should report to ICE (HSI) since it's immigrant-related."

I hear all of these. These are not case-ending problems.

Here's what I want attorneys new to T visa practice to understand immediately: the law enforcement certification — what we call I-914 Supplement B — is entirely optional. Congress built that in, and the 2024 final regulations and USCIS T Visa Policy Manual reinforce it clearly. USCIS does not require a Supplement B "T cert" signed by law enforcement to approve a T visa.

If you've ever hit a wall trying to get a U visa certification signed by a reluctant local agency, stop right now before you carry that same frustration into T visa practice, because the frameworks are genuinely different. The T visa is more attorney-driven, more client-centered, and frankly more forgiving of uncooperative law enforcement than the U visa ever was. If you're law enforcement reading this book, I don't mean to hurt your feelings. A T cert can still be really helpful, and we want law enforcement to hear us, to issue incident reports, to be kind and trauma-informed, and to sign T certs for cases, even ones that have to be reported long after the chances of prosecution are over. However, since that often is not our experience as immigration attorneys, the focus here is what to do when the LEA is not helping us.

What the regulations actually contemplate is this: a survivor can report trafficking to law enforcement — federal, state, local, even tribal — and file a T visa with evidence of that report, even if law enforcement never generates a proper incident report, never investigates, never certifies anything. The FBI, for example, rarely produces incident reports in the way local agencies do, and even when they do, the FBI does not provide us with those documents as a matter of, as I understand, federal agency policy. Homeland Security Investigations operates differently still. What matters is that a reasonable attempt at reporting was made, or that reporting is excused entirely by a trauma or age exception.

Yes, in some rare cases, there are exceptions to the reporting-to-law-enforcement requirement in T visa cases. USCIS policy recognizes that some survivors face danger in reporting. Some are in jurisdictions where reporting to local law enforcement would itself create risk. Some T visa applicants are children, and the rules related to reporting for minors are different depending on circumstances and age.

Overall, though, I usually want to try to report the trafficking. It functions as strong evidence for my case, creates a clear procedural record, and puts the government on notice. If the client will allow us to report, after we go through a discussion of what I know about each particular law enforcement agency that has jurisdiction to receive a report, it avoids USCIS having to determine whether any trauma exception applies. From a client perspective, reporting, even at a minimal level, may help them feel better.

A case that has gone cold or a very old case — one where the trafficking happened years ago, where the business folded, where the trafficker is deceased — is still potentially a viable T visa case. There is no statute of limitations on filing for a T visa, and I have reported trafficking and then filed T cases decades after the trafficking ended. I was still in middle school when some of my clients were first trafficked.

If you send a letter to a law enforcement agency documenting that your client was trafficked, and they don't respond, or they respond dismissively, or they say they can't find the old record — document it. Keep copies and move forward with the rest of your casework.

Advocacy Tip: If you are reporting to a state or local law enforcement agency (LEA), you may include the trafficking statute from the appropriate state. State definitions of trafficking are often similar to the federal definition, but local/state LEAs will be more familiar with their specific state-law version. In North Carolina, I believe the state-law definition of trafficking/involuntary servitude is actually broader and more inclusive than the federal statute in some respects. Nevertheless we still must use the federal definition in our T visa arguments. Just be aware that you may communicate better as an advocate with local law enforcement if you are fluent in both state and federal law. As one North Carolina local (County) U/T certifier for a Sheriff's office explained to me, the local county sheriff's office doesn't issue incident reports or charge suspects with federal crimes. That particular county did not want to see a statute from the wrong jurisdiction and did not want to see repeated copies of the very long T visa policy manual in a T or U certification request. They work in state statutes, and anything else submitted was viewed as extraneous or even esoteric. While taskforces may include both state, local and federal employees with overlapping jurisdictions and interests in both state and federal law, it is often the case that with local or state law enforcement, your focus should be mostly on state law if you are trying to push for T visa certification and/or criminal charges to be brought. If they show interest, you may have additional communications later referencing federal law or more specifics.

The T visa certification (I-914 Supp B) is helpful when you can get it from law enforcement. Often we prepare the draft "T cert" as part of our request to law enforcement if they are an agency that is helpful, but other agencies (such as U.S. DOL) would likely prefer you to leave such drafts out as they do their own form-filling if they will certify. If a T visa certification doesn't quite fit the federal definition of trafficking but fits the state definition well, it can still help your T visa case (remember, T visa certification is not required; law enforcement support is helpful but optional).

An I-914 B T cert from an LEA is not the spine of the case. Your client's declaration is. I do wish more agencies would sign them, because it would make USCIS's job easier, help clear backlogs, and recognize the trauma our clients have faced. But it is not required.

> **Advocacy Tip:** Why should any agency sign a "T cert" if they are not required? My answer to this is that it is the right thing to do. I have done consultations for devastated people who thought they could not file for a T visa because the law enforcement agency was unsupportive and declined to sign a certification for them. If Congress intended to encourage more survivors to come forward and cooperate with requests from law enforcement, we want law enforcement to have a broad, inclusive view on who should be certified so that when the case the LEA "really wants" help on comes out, it is because it is already well known that others in the community (perhaps with less evidence) have been feeling safe and supportive enough to encourage others to report to a safe LEA.

The mechanics of this documenting reporting matter more than attorneys realize, and I've learned some of these lessons the hard way.

When you send a letter to a law enforcement agency on behalf of your client, send it in a way you can prove. FedEx with tracking. Certified mail with return receipt. An email to a confirmed address with a read or delivery receipt requested and a copy saved to your file immediately. I have had agencies claim they never received correspondence. Local detectives might say they don't know anything about any letter and find it a year later on another colleague's desk. Your proof of delivery is important for your T visa case.

And before you send anything, you do have the option to pick up the phone.

You can call the LEA, and you don't have to name your client. You don't have to disclose facts. You can simply ask: if someone wanted to report human trafficking to your department, what is the correct email address or mailing address to use? Who is the right person to receive that? Is there a designated trafficking unit or investigator? That one phone call — which takes maybe two minutes — means your formal letter lands somewhere it might actually be read, rather than sitting in a general mailbox that nobody monitors.

Document that call in your file notes. Write down who you spoke to, when, what they said, and what contact information they gave you. Then send your letter to that specific contact, at that specific address, and save your proof of delivery alongside those notes.

> **Pro Tip:** Do a short affidavit about your attempts to call or conversations with law enforcement that may otherwise not have a written record. You could get sick or leave a job, and the law firm will want that documentation. The saying of witness memories may fade and witnesses may go away, is relevant to your own work — if something were to happen to you would want the affidavit to have been done contemporaneously. This short affidavit may be useful someday to submit as evidence that you did in fact report, or simply as a way for your colleagues to pick up the threads if you move on or take leave from the firm.

This is not glamorous lawyering. It's the kind of administrative care that wins cases quietly, years later, when USCIS has a question and you have receipts.

Now, in terms of what USCIS is actually looking for when no T certification exists, the USCIS Policy Manual is worth understanding carefully. The manual explains that T visa applicants must show they are victims of a severe form of trafficking in persons — that framing encompasses both sex trafficking and labor trafficking, and the manual goes into detail about what those terms mean in practice. It addresses the "force, fraud, or coercion" elements. It addresses what "induced" means in the context of commercial sex acts. It explains that the applicant must be physically present in the US, a port of entry, or a qualifying territory or possession to file.

The manual is also where you find the most useful language about the "reason to believe" standard USCIS uses to evaluate whether the applicant is a victim. This is not a beyond-a-reasonable-doubt analysis. This is not even a preponderance standard in the traditional adversarial sense. USCIS is asking whether, based on all the evidence presented, there is a credible basis to believe this person was trafficked. That is a workable standard for a well-developed declaration supported by corroborating evidence.

The manual addresses what qualifies as corroborating evidence when law enforcement documentation is absent or thin. It contemplates statements from service providers, medical records, social worker assessments, psychological evaluations, photos, pay stubs, records of debt, records of movement, news articles about a specific trafficking operation — the universe of what can corroborate a declaration is genuinely broad.

It also addresses what happens when an applicant has less corroboration than we would prefer. USCIS is supposed to consider the totality of the circumstances and recognize that trafficking survivors often cannot produce the same documentary trail that other immigration applicants can. The manual says that directly.

So, when you're building the no-certification case, your roadmap is in two places: your client's declaration, and the T Visa Policy Manual. The T visa regulations and statute are critical resources, but often the T Visa Policy Manual is the go-to document for adjudicators.

The Core Four (Evidence for a T Visa)

When immigration lawyers first start looking into T visas, they often experience a moment of panic because the case may initially appear to lack evidence. Let me reassure you that it is usually not as bad as you think.

The Core Four: There are four main types of evidence you want (Victim Declaration, Proof of Reporting, Physical Presence Evidence, TVAP Referral).

We are so conditioned by other areas of immigration law to expect that we need a mountain of objective, third-party, irrefutable proof with DNA and a video and eye-witnesses (we don't). We think we need a neat, pre-packaged police report signed by the Chief of Police (we don't, though I do love it when I get one). We think we need a criminal conviction, or a stack of paystubs spanning three years, or a signed confession from the employer (we don't). We assume that if we don't have a signed law enforcement "T visa certification" (i.e., the Form I-914, Supplement B) that the case is dead on arrival.

Set those assumptions aside. The victim declaration is the evidentiary anchor, not paystubs or a conviction.

The T visa is a humanitarian benefit governed by the "any credible evidence" standard. The regulations explicitly state that the burden is on the applicant to demonstrate eligibility by a preponderance of the evidence, and to do so, the applicant "may submit any credible evidence relating to a T nonimmigrant application for consideration by USCIS." USCIS does not require a formal investigation or prosecution to be initiated. USCIS, not the law enforcement agency, has the final say on whether your client is a victim of a severe form of trafficking (unless they deny a case, in which case, the AAO or a federal judge might decide!).

I always thought it was so odd that the U visa program requires a U cert to be signed by law enforcement, but the T program made it optional. Yet, having spoken to many professionals who constantly dispute what trafficking is, and having seen the profound trauma individuals experience when reporting something that happened 30 years ago, I understand why lawmakers intentionally designed T certs to be optional.

But "any credible evidence" is a broad, abstract legal concept. What does that actually look like when you are assembling a filing packet?

Filing a T visa without evidence is obviously not okay, but I think some lawyers and clients don't realize that the evidence for T visa cases is usually forward-looking. This means that there are things you have to do with your client now, to document the past. So, the evidence we use is often much more accessible and holistic than lawyers realize. You do not need to build a criminal prosecutor's trial binder. Instead, you need to focus on the **Core Four**.

If you have these four main types of evidence, you have the foundation of a highly persuasive, winnable T visa case:

1. The Victim Declaration (well written and honest)
2. Proof of Reporting (might be an email or a letter with delivery confirmation)
3. Physical Presence Evidence (therapy, medical treatment)
4. TVAP Referral (often a resource list or if lucky, some financial/social support)

Anything else you get — the text messages from the abusive boss, the photos of the unsafe roofing site, the medical bills for the untreated injury — may also be helpful. Of course we always ask our clients if they might have old texts, or do they still have a scar from what happened, or are there old paystubs or a photo of the worksite. Gather what you can, but keep in mind that many trafficking victims simply don't have those things, either because traffickers try to make sure they won't or due to passage of time.

Let's break down the Core Four some more.

1. The Victim Declaration (The Heart of the Case)

The victim declaration truly is the heart of the T visa case.

The 2024 regulations are incredibly clear about this requirement. Under 8 CFR 214.204(c), initial evidence for a T visa application *must* include:

"A detailed, signed personal statement from the applicant, in their own words, addressing: (i) The circumstances surrounding the applicant's victimization... (ii) How the applicant's physical presence in the United States relates to the trafficking; (iii) The hardship, including harm or mistreatment the applicant fears if they are removed from the United States; and (iv) Whether they have complied with any reasonable law enforcement request for assistance..."

This document is where you may win or lose your case. It is the primary vehicle through which USCIS will understand what happened. It may be more important than your legal brief. It is not something I believe should be handwritten or without attorney review, especially because the regulation wants certain magic words included, such as the ones about complying with any reasonable law enforcement request for assistance. I wish it were different and that people could apply more easily, but the reality is that the statement, if deficient, will not pass muster. So this is where your efforts should go, and often, if you are taking on an initial T visa case or a type of case that is unfamiliar to you, you will want to pair up with another person who is able to mentor you through this process. One reason I host guest speakers at our CLE program is to encourage mentoring (paid or free) among T visa advocates. Especially with solo practitioners, having a mentor and someone else to review a T visa case before filing can be a game-changer (as always, rules related to confidentiality, ethics, and co-counsel, apply).

What USCIS Needs to Know Most When drafting this statement, you have to stay focused on the adjudicator's needs. USCIS officers are reading hundreds of these. They need you to connect the dots. The declaration should be relentlessly focused on three main things:

1. **The Trafficking Victimization:** You should clearly articulate the *action*, the *means*, and the *purpose*. How was the client recruited, harbored, or transported? What were the force, fraud, or coercion tactics used by the trafficker? How did those tactics result in involuntary servitude or a commercial sex act? Focus

on **"Trafficker Active Voice"** to ensure the narrative highlights the perpetrator's actions rather than the client's self-blame. For instance, instead of "I *forced myself* to go back to work while injured because otherwise I wouldn't have food to eat and I'd get fired," the statement might read, "*My trafficker made me* to go back to work while injured, saying they'd fire me if I didn't come back now." Why? Because the trafficker used threats of financial harm and unlawful termination to coerce the victim to return to work while still injured. The worker did not coerce himself. Maybe the worker was trying to say, it took all their strength (emotional and physical) to physically get to work, and that's where the phrase "I forced myself" came from. Clarifying what the worker was trying to tell you should be done as part of the victim statement drafting and communication process with your client, before a final declaration is signed. You want an accurate representation of the victimization.

2. **How the Person is Getting Help:** This is vital. You want to document how the client is stabilizing and healing. Are they seeing a therapist? Have they gone to physical therapy for the hand they injured on the job site? Are they accessing community resources? This directly feeds into their physical presence and extreme hardship arguments. What if they aren't getting any help? Well, that's where a good attorney is going to refer them for help to a real professional. We take time to ask what might help them the most – is it physical therapy for a workplace injury? Is it tattoo removal or modification because the trafficker put their name on the victim's arm as a brand? Is it varicose vein surgery to stop the pain and burning the client feels due to being made to stand for 18-hour shifts under

threat of deportation for so many years? Our particular law office has been fortunate in that the Masters in Social Work program at our local university places their MSW students in the field with us, so we have people who know what resources are out there and can help us get referrals for help for our clients.

3. **Why They Need to Remain in the US:** You should explicitly connect their current presence to trafficking. This means explaining the ongoing trauma, the need for continued medical or mental health care that isn't available in their home country, or their ongoing cooperation with an investigation. The T Visa Policy Manual (updated recently) has a wonderful list of things you can ask about. So don't go rogue. Ask about those things. Don't distract the USCIS officer with unnecessary information.

The Attorney's Ethical Obligation: Read It and Proofread

Drafting a declaration is an iterative, collaborative, and trauma-informed process. It is not something you can outsource completely to a paralegal, nor is it something you should simply ask the client to write and then submit unedited. The new T visa regulations are not written at a level people without a legal education can easily grasp.

As the attorney of record, you are expected to have truly read and proofread the victim statement. You are looking for mathematical plausibility — ensuring the timeline, the hours worked, and the wages stolen actually make sense and align with the client's travel history. USCIS does not like discrepancies, so find them and figure out why something is off. If your client says they escaped the trafficker in 2015, but their I-94 shows they traveled to Mexico and re-entered in 2016 with the trafficker, you need to clarify that timeline before you file so it doesn't trigger a Request for Evidence (RFE). You should read the statement with a critical eye, ensuring it meets the statutory requirements while remaining true to the client's voice. Sometimes, things won't match up. We had a case years ago where we just had to respond and say we know this does not match up. This is the client's memory. These are the documents we have. Honesty mattered. Especially when trauma can impact memory, be aware that patience is required.

Freedom of Information Act (FOIA) requests with USCIS, EOIR, CBP, and OBIM offices, as well as FBI background checks, should help you obtain prior immigration and criminal history for your client to complete a discrepancy review. For many clients who have complex immigration histories, we must "frontload" the submission of the FOIA and other record requests early on, so that we do not finalize a final victim statement without knowing what is on record. For example, if a FOIA reveals a December of 1999 removal order but the statement draft referenced January of 2000, it may be a simple discrepancy to resolve by addressing those records with your client.

The Interpreter and Translator Certification This is a non-negotiable ethical and procedural standard: if your client's best language is not English, the declaration should be interpreted or translated by a competent professional, and a certification of interpretation/translation should be included.

Never use a client's family member to translate the declaration. First, it is an enormous ethical risk regarding client autonomy and confidentiality. Second, family members often filter, soften, or alter the trauma the client is expressing because it is too painful for them to hear, or because of cultural shame. Use a professional interpreter to read the finalized English statement back to the client in their native language to ensure they completely understand and agree with every single word before they sign it.

Include a standard certification block at the bottom of a translation. For example: *"I, [translator name], certify that I am competent to translate from [foreign language] to English and that the foregoing is a complete and accurate translation of the attached document."*

An interpreter certification might be: *"I, [interpreter name], certify that I am fluent in both English and [Language]and that I am competent to translate and interpret from English to [Language] and from [Language] to English. I further certify that I read the entire declaration to the Applicant, [applicant name], in [Language], a language the Applicant understands. The Applicant confirmed that they understood the contents of the declaration before signing it. My interpretation of the declaration from English to [Language] was true, complete, and accurate to the best of my abilities."*

2. Proof of Reporting (Compliance with Law Enforcement)

The second piece of the Core Four is proof that your client has complied with reasonable requests for assistance from law enforcement.

This is the element that historically causes the most panic for immigration lawyers. You might say we are a jumpy bunch! When we have found a trafficking victim, we want to do no harm. We have been conditioned by the U visa process to believe that we must secure a signed certification from a police chief or a district attorney.

Let's look at what the 2024 T visa regulation says about this. 8 CFR 214.208(b) states:

"An applicant must, at a minimum, contact an LEA [Law Enforcement Agency] with proper jurisdiction to report the acts of a severe form of trafficking in persons. Credible evidence documenting a single contact with an LEA may suffice. Reporting may be telephonic, electronic, or through other means."

Read that again: *Credible evidence documenting a single contact with an LEA may suffice...*

The regulations do not require an active investigation. They do not require an arrest. They do not require a criminal conviction. The decision to pursue an investigation or prosecution falls solely within the discretion of law enforcement. Your job as the immigration lawyer is to make the report on behalf of your client and to document their willingness to cooperate if the agency decides to act.

Soft vs. Hard Reporting In practice, you will strategically decide where to report the trafficking based on the facts of the case and the safety of your client. Do your research about which agencies have the power to detect, investigate or prosecute the trafficking (in theory) based on where the trafficking victimization took place.

- **"Soft" Reporting:** This often involves reporting the trafficking to an agency that is trauma informed, that will understand you are doing your best to document your client's victimization, and which will not request unreasonable levels of cooperation. Many agencies will receive a report and do nothing further. Some have a rule that the trafficker will not be alerted as to who reported unless a criminal action moves forward.

- **"Hard" Reporting or Case Already Active:** This involves reporting in cases where you think there might be a high interest in investigating and even making an arrest. Sometimes, a case will come to us referred by law enforcement for help. The case might be ongoing in criminal court.

Whichever you choose, make sure that the client understands that at some point it is possible that they will have to talk to the law enforcement agency about what happened, but that you will do your best to make sure it happens in a reasonable and trauma-informed way. Just as we cannot guarantee an approval, we can't guarantee that they'll never have to talk to a law enforcement agency. As the advocate, though, you can do your research based on your trauma-informed assessment of the case and client and make legally sufficient but careful choices.

What is the "Proof"? If a signed LEA Declaration (Supplement B) is entirely optional, what does your "Proof of Reporting" actually look like in the filing packet?

It is often incredibly simple documentary evidence. If you report the trafficking to the FBI's National Threat Operations Center (NTOC) via their electronic tip form, your proof is the screenshot of the final page that says "Submission Successful" along with a copy of the narrative you pasted into the web form. You might follow up with a letter or email or phone call, but the FBI may decline to talk to you about it.

If you report to the Department of Labor or a local police department via email, your proof is the printed email showing the date, time, and the agency address you sent it to. If you send a formal reporting letter via FedEx to the local District Attorney, your proof is the copy of the letter and the FedEx delivery confirmation receipt.

You include this documentation in the application packet and explain in the client's declaration: *"I have worked with my attorney to provide the relevant information so that they could report the trafficking to law enforcement on my behalf. A copy of that documentation will be included in my application. I am willing and able to comply with reasonable requests to assist law enforcement."*

If the agency never calls you back, or if they reply and say, "we lack the resources to investigate this," that is fine. You have met the requirement of reporting, and you have the evidence to prove it. If they say this isn't trafficking, you may need to step up and advocate some more. But you're not required to change an official's mind at the local level.

Note: There are statutory exceptions to this requirement. If the client was under 18 at the time of the trafficking, or if they suffer from physical or psychological trauma that prevents cooperation, they are exempt from reporting. In those cases, your "proof" may be evidence of their age or a psychological evaluation documenting the severe trauma. That said, there are reasons to report anyway, so for situations where you're not sure, talk to a mentor.

3. Physical Presence Evidence

The third pillar of the Core Four is proving that your client is physically present in the United States *on account of* the trafficking.

This is another area where the 2024 regulations brought massive, practitioner-friendly clarifications. Historically, adjudicators and lawyers alike misunderstood this requirement. A common myth was that the trafficker must have literally smuggled or brought the victim across the U.S. border. That myth confused so many people.

Rather than requiring that the trafficker have brought the person into the US, the law requires that the applicant be physically present in the U.S. on account of the trafficking *at the time of the application*. For example, a client could have entered the U.S. perfectly legally on a student visa ten years ago, or crossed the border voluntarily seeking work, and then fallen victim to labor trafficking in a restaurant in North Carolina three years later.

Furthermore, the 2024 regulations explicitly state that the passage of time alone does not negate an applicant's ability to establish physical presence. The regulations also provide broad protections for clients who may have departed the U.S. after the trafficking but later returned. For example, new 8 CFR 214.207(b)(5) allows an applicant who departed to satisfy physical presence if they "*returned to the United States and received treatment or services related to their victimization that cannot be provided in their home country or last place of residence outside the United States.*"

How Do You Actually Prove This? You can prove physical presence by showing how the client is stabilizing, recovering, and receiving help in the United States today, or explaining how they have been identified (or self-identified) as a trafficking victim and have begun to receive help.

The 2024 regulations at 8 CFR 214.207(c) provide a fantastic, non-exhaustive list of what this evidence looks like. It includes:

"(2) Affidavits, evaluations, diagnoses, or other records from the applicant's service providers (including therapists, psychologists, psychiatrists, and social workers) documenting the therapeutic, psychological, or medical services the applicant has sought or is currently accessing as a result of victimization and that describe how the applicant's life is being impacted by the trauma at the time of filing and describing any mental health conditions resulting from the trafficking."

Connecting clients to the help they need relates to establishing physical presence on account of trafficking.

When you screen a client and uncover trafficking, one of your first steps should be assessing their physical and mental health. Do they have symptoms of severe, debilitating anxiety or PTSD from the sexual harassment and coercion they faced at the motel? Connect them with a licensed clinical social worker or psychologist. Do they have severe, chronic back pain or a loss of mobility in their hand because their roofing boss denied them safety equipment and forced them to work through an injury? Connect them with a doctor or a physical therapist.

Your physical presence evidence is the Treatment Report from that clinical social worker detailing the client's diagnosis of PTSD and their ongoing need for trauma-informed cognitive behavioral therapy. Your evidence is the letter from the physical therapist outlining the exercises required to manage the client's chronic pain.

When you submit these medical and psychological records, you are telling USCIS a clear, documented story: My client is in the United States today because they are receiving critical care to heal from the trauma of human trafficking — care that they would lose access to if they were deported to their home country.

These records do double-duty for the T visa application. They simultaneously satisfy both the "Physical Presence" requirement and the "Extreme Hardship" requirement.

One more thing about therapy. I don't particularly love one-time one-session evaluations, and USCIS hasn't seemed to give sufficient weight to them unless the client also followed the psychologist's recommendation to attend therapy thereafter. I have seen Requests for Evidence related to that issue — essentially USCIS argued that if the person was diagnosed with PTSD due to trafficking and needed to remain in the U.S. to receive treatment, they should actually be receiving the treatment and not just showing a document that says they need help. Years ago we saw situations where someone only started going to therapy after the RFE was issued, and then with a decision (denial) or second RFE, USCIS highlighted this in a very negative way. This is unfortunate because often it takes a long time to connect people to therapy and often we are seeking therapists with specialization in trafficking trauma, specific languages (e.g. Mam, Gujarati, Czech), coordinating interpreters, and working to find providers clients can afford.

While a person's need for therapy or services should be enough for USCIS, as a practical matter, receiving ongoing needed assistance (which both client and therapist independently agree is helpful), and documenting those ongoing services, may avoid an unfair accusation or RFE that drifts into questions about whether the person who attested to needing therapy in the declaration, actually has taken any steps to receive help.

The ongoing attendance/ongoing therapy sessions documenting the need to receive mental health services may be a better way to help your client and also prove your case. Cost-wise, a person might go into treatment and get in many sessions of therapy compared to the cost of an expensive one-time evaluation, so treatment summaries are often more affordable.

A local non-profit called me once and asked if we wanted both since it would be free — and for that I said yes. But that was because it would mean our client would get the counseling they really needed, not only a letter saying they need counseling.

Please forgive me for the practicality of some of my suggestions. In an ideal world, USCIS would grant the work permit and T status immediately so that the client could afford evaluations, therapy, and even more services, easily. Since that is not the current reality, we are in the cycle of trying to find services our clients can use to get the real mental health assistance they need before filing a case with USCIS and while it's pending, while USCIS seems to want to see the person already has those things to more easily approve the case.

And that brings me to the TVAP program, which in theory could be the bridge we need — a way to get help for T visa clients before they even apply for a T visa.

While therapy is not a requirement to win a T visa case, the above illustration is intended to highlight how the TVAP program is supposed to help trafficking survivors with receiving assistance and also how it should help document that the client is receiving trafficking related assistance, when USCIS policy and regulation indicate that receiving help is a piece of evidence for a T visa case. It's critical for TVAP providers to be well-funded so they can help survivors of trafficking and document the help the survivor is receiving.

4. TVAP Referral (Trafficking Victim Assistance Program)

The final piece of the Core Four is the TVAP referral.

The Trafficking Victim Assistance Program (TVAP) is a federal grant program administered by the Department of Health and Human Services (HHS) that funds comprehensive case management services for foreign national victims of trafficking through a national network of service providers.

When you identify a trafficking survivor, your law firm can make a referral to the local TVAP agency in your client's state. This program can provide incredible "wraparound services" for your client, including limited financial assistance for rent and utilities, grocery support, job training, and funding to pay for the very therapy and medical care we just discussed in the Physical Presence section. T visa applicants are not subject to the public charge ground of inadmissibility, so it helps to discuss that with your client. Also, as a practical matter of communication, we want to explain we are not "referring the client out" (this may mislead them into thinking we are not taking their case or are ending representation), but rather, we are requesting that the TVAP program provide them with some help while we are going to represent them as attorneys in the T visa application process. This may be the first time ever that a survivor finds out about the TVAP program, so it takes a bit of time to explain it. Most people are very receptive and incredibly glad to get support.

So, this sounds perfect, right? Unfortunately, a lot of non-profits have lost funding recently, and so the number of people who actually are connected with the free social worker to get this financial and other wraparound help is limited.

Sometimes we just get a local community resource list in response to a TVAP request for connection, but wow — sometimes it's been super helpful.

I can think of many clients who loved the help they got locally and felt very supported.

One reason traffickers successfully abuse people is they are really good at isolating people and making them feel like there is no one to help them. Getting community support for your client isn't just good evidence – it's life changing to help someone feel less alone, more loved, more financially stable.

Why is this a Core Evidence piece? Submitting proof of a TVAP referral and any service or resource list received is evidence that your client has accessed some service or benefit as a result of being trafficked.

Look again at the 2024 regulations regarding physical presence. 8 CFR 214.207(c)(3) explicitly states that USCIS will consider:

"Documentation of any stabilizing services and benefits, including financial, language, housing, or legal resources, the applicant is accessing or has accessed as a result of being trafficked."

Your evidentiary "proof" for this pillar is incredibly straightforward. It is a copy of the email sent to the regional TVAP coordinator.

For example, your evidence might literally be an email that says: "Hi TVAP team, I have a new referral for TVAP services. The client is a male labor trafficking survivor located in [City]. A T-visa application is being prepared. He needs financial assistance for rent, utilities, and paying for trauma therapy. Please let us know if an agency is available to assist him." You'll find that there's a PDF form that will be emailed back to you to complete for USCRI. You'll send that in and get a response back, hopefully either connecting your client to trafficking-related services (help) or at least providing a local resource list. The PDF form does not require that you provide an extensive description of trafficking but rather, one sentence is sufficient (e.g. They were a victim of labor trafficking in Boston.)

By including this email in your filing packet, you are providing contemporaneous, documentary proof that your client is actively accessing or requesting stabilizing services in the United States as a result of being trafficked. It proves they are establishing a support network. It proves they are seeking rehabilitation. USCIS adjudicators should be pleased to see that a victim is connected to a recognized federal support network.

Can you imagine reading T visa cases at the USCIS office all day? Show them how coordinated, trauma-informed legal advocacy empowers clients and helps them rebuild their lives.

Even if the TVAP agency is currently out of funding and places the client on a waitlist, the *attempt* to access these stabilizing services demonstrates the client's ongoing need to remain in the United States to recover from their victimization.

There is no cost to refer someone to a TVAP program, but it can be life changing.

We manage expectations about how much help a TVAP program might provide, and when we get a "community resource list" instead of a connection to a social worker from a TVAP provider, we at least have provided a starting point for more community support of the client.

To learn more about the TVAP program you can look at USCRI's website: https://refugees.org/trafficking/

The Extra Evidence vs. The Core Four

When you are building your case, do not get bogged down worrying about the evidence you *don't* have.

Traffickers do not usually provide their victims with W-2s, detailed contracts, or written threats (although when their checks bounce, we might get that from the bank!). If you are lucky enough to have a client who managed to save text messages from the trafficker, photos of the unsafe work conditions, paystubs proving wage theft, or hospital records from the day of an assault — use them! That is fantastic corroborating evidence (assuming you review the paychecks and they do not contradict or confuse the matter).

But if you don't have those things, do not panic. The absence of "perfect" evidence should not deter you from filing a good case for a deserving survivor.

If you have a meticulously proofread, trauma-informed Victim Declaration that focuses on the victimization and the need for help; if you have the email showing Proof of Reporting to a law enforcement agency; if you have Physical Presence Evidence in the form of a therapist's letter; and if you have the email showing a TVAP Referral — you have built a legally sound T visa application.

You have met the "any credible evidence" standard, and you have given USCIS what they need to approve the case and change your client's life.

Still anxious? I know, we're a nervous bunch. It's ok. You can always keep working on gathering more evidence in case of an RFE (Request for Evidence). For example, your client might have receipts from monthly therapy sessions, or you might get a T cert signed after your case has been pending with USCIS for a while, or maybe you'll find some news stories later. I've had some "wow" moments when we located criminal histories on traffickers and found out that their threats of violence to our client were not all they had done — but in fact, a trafficker had already been to prison before for violent crimes. Public records and the internet and looking up whether a business has been sued or has a bunch of reviews online about not paying its workers, might help to show a scheme, pattern or plan.

As long as the T visa case remains pending with USCIS, you can send additional evidence, or if you get an RFE, use it to respond at that time.

Remember, this is the T visa framework. You, your team, and your client, are building the case with the materials you have based on your client's specific history and needs. You can and should customize your case plan.

Practitioner Tip: You can use paystubs, texts, court transcripts, affidavits regarding prosecution assistance, conviction records, or photos as great bonus evidence. Or you can hold onto it to see if it will be useful later. I would resist the urge to include hundreds of pages of extraneous evidence in a filing.

How to Use Corroborating Evidence

When you sit down to assemble a T visa packet, your foundation will likely be the Core Four. If you have a well-written, accurate, truthful victim declaration, proof of reporting, physical presence evidence, and a TVAP referral, you have the foundation of a highly persuasive, winnable case. You have met the necessary burden of proof, and you have given USCIS the tools they need to approve the application. However, there will be times when a client walks into your office and hands you a piece of documentary evidence that perfectly corroborates their story, or there will be days when you yourself find information about the trafficker (often online). For example, for a client who cannot remember the last name of their boss, we might find the name online on the State incorporation records website since the boss was a registered agent of the business. There, we may find names of others involved in the company, to ask the client questions about.

A Cantina Hypothetical: Uncovering the Evidence

Let us look at how this plays out in a real-world scenario involving a nightlife establishment. Cantinas, bars, and clubs are environments where trafficking frequently hides in plain sight. These cases can be especially difficult for lawyers to recognize at first because they often sit at the intersection of labor exploitation, sexual coercion, and social pressure. Let us imagine a consultation with a young woman named Monica who was recruited to work as a waitress at a local cantina.

Monica was promised a stable job serving drinks with the opportunity to earn good tips. Once she began working, the expectations quickly expanded. The manager imposed strict drink quotas and required her to sit with intoxicated customers for hours at a time. If Monica didn't encourage customers to buy expensive drinks, the manager cut her shifts or started making "jokes" about deporting her for not selling enough of the good stuff. Eventually, the pressure from management escalated dramatically. Customers began expecting sexual contact after spending large amounts of money at the bar. The manager made it implicitly clear that refusing these requests would jeopardize her job and the employer-provided housing she relied on. Monica felt completely trapped because her livelihood, housing, and immigration safety depended entirely on complying with these sexual demands.

Using the Extra Evidence to Build the Case

In Monica's situation, she never called the police because she was terrified of deportation. When she finally escapes and comes to your office for a consultation, she feels like she has absolutely no proof of what happened to her. But as you conduct your trauma-informed screening, you ask her if she happened to save any messages or take any pictures while she worked at the cantina. It turns out Monica has a wealth of extra evidence hidden on her cell phone. She has WhatsApp messages from the manager explicitly stating that if she did not keep a high-paying customer happy in the back room, it was "not gonna be good for her" (which she took to mean there would be severe consequences). She also took a photograph of the employee whiteboard in the back office showing the mandatory daily drink quotas and the penalties for failing to meet them. Finally, she has screenshots of cash transfer apps showing she was forced to pay a "house fee" directly to the manager every time a customer tipped her.

This extra evidence can be helpful for a T visa application. You will prepare and proofread a victim declaration where Monica truthfully explains the timeline and the coercion she faced. You can attach printed, certified translations of the WhatsApp messages to corroborate the trafficker's abuse of the legal process (i.e., coercion). You can include the photograph of the whiteboard to prove the coercive commission structure and the excessive demands. You may attach the cash app receipts to demonstrate the financial control and economic abuse. You should not need a signed law enforcement certification ("T cert") to win this case, because you have an overwhelming narrative of coercion.

What happens if law enforcement actually wants an interview? There are cases where we have received referrals from law enforcement or the National Human Trafficking Hotline knowing we handle T visa cases, and of course those would be more active cases. There are times when we do get a request for an interview. I have, for example, attended many U.S. DOL interviews (in-person before the pandemic, and later, by phone). Those usually last about 2 hours. If you handle phone calls, or a phone-based or video interview, you should be taking notes and later on, preparing an affidavit that summarizes your client's cooperation with reasonable requests related to the interview. If you have emails about coordinating the date and time for an interview, save those as possible extra evidence.

I save business cards from detectives. I save phone messages my staff wrote down to call back FBI agents. If my client has a police report related to the trafficker, but it wasn't a trafficking report, I might save it or I might use it for the T visa case.

Regarding preparing for the interview, I have hosted CLEs where we invite former prosecutors and retired FBI agent(s) or even current law enforcement agency officers to join and teach. This helps us learn more about what they want to see in an interview, and how to prepare. The more law enforcement we speak to, the more we realize they have vastly different preferences related to how we should communicate with them. That is something worth mentioning as whatever experience you have with one LEA may not necessarily prepare you for the next, but can act as guidance.

Formatting Your Bonus Evidence for USCIS

When you submit this extra evidence, it is your job to make it as easy as possible for the USCIS adjudicator to understand its significance. You should not dump a stack of unorganized text messages or blurry photographs into the back of your T-1 filing packet. If you submit text messages or WhatsApp records in a foreign language, you must provide a certified English translation for them, and the messages should be relevant to your T visa case. If you submit photographs of an injury or a worksite, you should print them clearly and include a short caption underneath explaining what the photo depicts and the date it was taken.

You must explicitly connect this extra evidence back to the legal elements of human trafficking in your attorney cover letter. You will use your cover letter to explain how the text messages demonstrate "threats of serious harm" or "abuse of the legal process." You will explain how the paystubs or financial records demonstrate a "scheme, plan, or pattern intended to cause a person to believe that failure to perform an act would result in serious harm." By combining the Core Four elements with this organized additional evidence, you give the adjudicator the credible evidence they need to comfortably approve the case and change your client's life.

What To Do When You're Told It's Not Trafficking, But You Have Your Core Four.

Well, you're probably going to file your T visa case anyway if you have followed the law and regulations. When you start filing T visas, you will eventually hit a wall where someone with seeming authority tells you that your case is not human trafficking, and that might make you wonder yet again, do you have enough evidence? It might be a local detective who reads your report and dismisses it as a simple labor dispute. It might be a prosecutor who tells you there is not enough evidence to pursue criminal charges or who says they are sick of people asking for victim visa certifications. It might even be another immigration attorney or a non-profit employee who is overly judgmental about who "deserves" to file a case.

It's hard when people in positions of authority tell new practitioners something wrong and even harder knowing that standards of adjudication or trends can morph over time. New-to-T-visa lawyers faced with any criticism often panic and assume their case is completely dead. You need to take a deep breath and remember that you are the immigration lawyer advocating for your client, and you may simply understand trafficking better than they do *even if you are new to this*. When I teach my classes "Is this a T Visa?" I try not to put myself above others or say that something is impossible. I try to just ask more questions to see if we legitimately can get to yes and to flag issues to develop upon if an attorney decides to take the T visa case.

Gatekeepers. A gatekeeper is someone who positions themselves as the final authority on whether a case qualifies — and then uses that authority to shut cases down rather than develop them.

Here's how you spot one. They speak in absolutes. "That's not trafficking." "USCIS will never approve that." "You need a signed T cert or it's pointless." They may talk down to you rather than encourage dialogue or say "no" without a single follow-up question.

If they look at you blankly when you mention the 2024 regulations, you may be getting very confident advice from someone operating on very old information.

Gatekeepers are not always wrong. Sometimes they flag a real problem. But their certainty should give you pause, not paralysis. Your job is to assess the evidence you actually have, apply the current legal standard, and make a reasoned professional judgment. For example, I will see responses like "on these facts, no, this will never work." But where are the follow up questions, like "did you screen other jobs they had to see if there may have been problems there, or ask about gaps in employment? Or did you ask about ____ (something relevant)?" If someone is shutting you down without asking more helpful questions, consider a second opinion. They might be tired, or burned out, or simply unable to spend time or resources on your questions, and so it's worth trying to see if someone else professional has time and space to help you with a deep analysis before you proceed with your T visa case.

Law enforcement gatekeepers. Law enforcement agencies evaluate cases through the lens of criminal prosecution, not through a T visa lawyer lens. They are looking for evidence that can prove a crime beyond a reasonable doubt in front of a jury. They are also dealing with limited budgets, overburdened departments, and shifting internal prosecutorial priorities. Many officers have only been trained to recognize dramatic, movie-style sex trafficking scenarios involving minors, leaving them completely unequipped to recognize complex labor trafficking or smuggling-turned-trafficking cases.

USCIS immigration adjudicators, on the other hand, must evaluate cases through the humanitarian framework governing T visas using a preponderance of the evidence standard. These are two different systems with completely different goals, and a rejection from one does not dictate the outcome of the other. The burden of proof for a T visa is only slightly more than 50% — a preponderance of the evidence — at USCIS. A criminal conviction (i.e., beyond a reasonable doubt) might be something like 99% certainty needed. However, a criminal conviction requires proof beyond a reasonable doubt, which is exponentially higher than the preponderance of the evidence standard. Often what is enough for a T visa would not rise to the level of proof required to obtain a criminal conviction.

Consider a worker who falls off a roof and is forced back to work the next day under the threat of being blacklisted. A local patrol officer responding to a complaint might just see a workers' compensation issue or an undocumented immigrant working illegally. They may not be looking at the nuanced dynamics of how the employer abused the legal process to compel labor. But USCIS adjudicators can understand the trafficking and approve the T visa case if you make it clear to them.

Similarly, in a domestic violence scenario, police officers are usually looking for physical assault marks to make an immediate arrest. They may not be evaluating whether the abuser used that violence to trap the victim in a condition of domestic servitude or force them into commercial sex acts. Because their focus is entirely different, you cannot rely on their initial impressions to determine the viability of your immigration strategy. Triage is different from a comprehensive analysis, so when you are told you don't have enough evidence or your case is "unfounded," that might just mean it does not have enough to move forward to criminal charges. That does not mean your client is not qualified for a T visa.

You should remember that the immigration system does not require a successful criminal prosecution for a T visa case to succeed. The regulations require that the applicant comply with reasonable requests for assistance from law enforcement. The law does not require an active investigation, an arrest, or a signed law enforcement certification to establish eligibility. If you properly report the trafficking to an agency and they reply stating they lack the resources to investigate or do not see a crime, you have still met your requirement. If they don't even reply to you, you have still met your requirement (though I do appreciate at least a little bone being thrown like, "Received."). Regardless, you simply document your report, document your client's willingness to cooperate, and move forward with your filing.

This is why understanding your reporting options is so crucial. If a local police department is hostile or closely intertwined with immigration enforcement, you do not have to subject your client to that environment to prove trafficking.

You can potentially utilize soft reporting by submitting a detailed complaint to the Department of Labor or utilizing the FBI's National Threat Operations Center tip line (don't do anonymous tips though). If the FBI sends an automated response or the Department of Labor never follows up, your legal obligation should be fulfilled. The purpose of the report is to ensure law enforcement has been notified, not to force victims into criminal proceedings they do not control. I have to give credit to the California Labor Commission for how well trained they are overall in trafficking. I don't expect everyone to be like that. I've seen beautiful T certs signed by local police, prosecutors, U.S. DOL...but that's not my expectation with T cases.

It is frustrating when professionals who should be helping victims end up tearing them down instead. You will encounter naysayers who insist your case does not qualify because the client initially agreed to be smuggled or because the abuse happened in the context of a domestic relationship. One trafficking taskforce person, who should have known better, refused to acknowledge trafficking even after a T visa was approved, saying the person's physical movement had not been restrained. For him, that was the bar. If you weren't tied up or tied down, you weren't trafficked.

Early in my career, there were so many people who insisted these complex cases were impossible, but I eventually realized many of those critics had simply never successfully handled or litigated these cases themselves. Sometimes, they gatekept themselves — being so afraid to file, they told people they weren't qualified.

You cannot let other people's lack of gumption or outdated knowledge dictate the trajectory of your client's life. Do not be afraid to seek out multiple opinions, pair with a mentor, and forge your own pathway into this work. I know it is hard because what you file today might have to wait 31 months or more for a decision to be handed down, but that is pretty common with many types of immigration cases. Whether we are working on a business immigration case or a T visa case, there are possibilities of unfair NTA issuance, enforcement, errors, changes in law or policy, and so many unknowns for us to keep in mind, but full paralysis and doing nothing, is also a choice.

So, what do you do when someone rejects your trafficking theory, but you and your client are still ready, with all these concerns, to move forward? You focus on drafting a meticulous, trauma-informed victim declaration that clearly articulates the force, fraud, or coercion used by the trafficker. You use the specific terminology from the USCIS Policy Manual to frame the narrative, translating the client's raw experience into the statutory elements adjudicators need to see. You gather your physical presence evidence, secure a TVAP referral, and construct a clear, ethically sound legal argument.

Ultimately, USCIS has the final say on whether your client is a victim of a severe form of trafficking, not the detective who didn't respond to your email. Even if USCIS were to deny the application, you may still file an appeal or motion with the AAO (USCIS Administrative Appeals Office), or in many cases, file an APA (Administrative Procedures Act) lawsuit in a federal U.S. district court challenging the denial. If your client is willing to let you fight for them, you can fight for them.

Self-Esteem Exercise

This chapter was a lot. I know.

Look at what you just absorbed: the Core Four, the reporting mechanics, the evidence packaging, the gatekeepers, the cantina hypothetical, the declaration drafting ethics.

Here's your exercise. Write down two trafficking indicators you would have missed before reading this book.

1.

2.

Then write down what you would do differently in a consultation tomorrow:

1.

2.

That's your growth. That's a real person who gets seen instead of sent away.

You are becoming the lawyer trafficking survivors need.

Chapter Five is where we move from building the case to filing it — the mechanics of the T-1 packet itself, common RFE triggers, and how to prepare your client for what comes after submission.

5

More Trafficking Scenarios (Now That You're Inspired)

Even if you're a business immigration lawyer, please don't skip this section. Sexual abuse is pervasive worldwide in every industry and socioeconomic class, and now we are going to talk about how it may apply in the T visa context.

Sex Trafficking Beyond Prostitution ("Thing of Value")

Commercial sex trafficking does not require an exchange of money. An abuser offering a victim their life, physical safety, or family unification in exchange for coerced sex acts constitutes a "thing of value."

When "Sex Trafficking" Does Not Look Like Sex Work

Sex trafficking does not always involve prostitution or sex work in the way people typically imagine it.

Many practitioners initially assume that sex trafficking requires some kind of organized commercial activity — advertisements, clients, or payments exchanged in an obvious way. But the law is broader than that, and in real practice the dynamics can look very different.

Sex trafficking can also occur within an intimate relationship and involve only two people. In these situations, the "thing of value" exchanged for the sexual act may not be money at all. Instead, it may be: the survivor's safety, the promise of a visa extension, continued visa sponsorship, continued housing, promises of immigration stability, drugs, alcohol, a promise to send money to family or to bring them to the U.S. Sometimes the "thing of value" is the victim's life (i.e., being allowed to keep living).

Consider the dynamic that sometimes develops in extremely violent relationships. An abusive partner may repeatedly threaten the survivor with physical harm. The survivor may understand very clearly that refusing the partner's demands could lead to serious violence. Over time, sexual acts occur not because the survivor freely consents, but because the alternative is the threat of harm.

From a legal perspective, the abusive partner is effectively making a coercive exchange: compliance in sexual acts in return for the temporary withholding of violence.

In other words, the survivor's safety becomes the "thing of value."

The abusive partner is implicitly offering something of value — the promise not to inflict harm — in exchange for sexual acts obtained through coercion. When viewed through the legal framework of trafficking law, that dynamic can fall within the definition of commercial sex trafficking, even though there is no brothel, no advertisement, and no outside customers.

For lawyers encountering this concept for the first time, it can feel counterintuitive. However, once you begin to recognize these patterns, it becomes easier to see how coercion within relationships can create situations where sexual acts are effectively forced through threats tied to something of value.

Understanding this principle is important because survivors themselves rarely describe their experiences in these legal terms. They may simply say that their partner demanded sex or that refusing felt too dangerous. They may not initially recognize that the law treats coercive sexual exploitation as a form of trafficking.

How Screening Questions Can Reveal the Pattern

This is one of the moments in a consultation where careful questioning can help reveal the broader picture.

For example, a lawyer might begin with relatively simple questions about the relationship:

1. Were there times when you felt you could not refuse to go to bed with him because you were afraid of what might happen?

2. Did your partner ever threaten violence or immigration consequences if you did not comply with their demands?

3. Did you ever feel that agreeing was the only way to stay safe in the moment?

At first, the answers to these questions may sound like descriptions of domestic violence/intimate partner violence, rather than trafficking. But as the conversation continues, the pattern can become clearer.

Hypo: H-4 spouse and "the thing of value"

Imagine a consultation where an H-4 spousal visa holder initially describes years of abuse by her H-1B spouse. She explains that he frequently threatened to harm her if she disobeyed him. During the conversation, the lawyer asks whether there were times when she felt pressured into sexual acts she did not want.

She hesitates and then explains that refusing was never really an option. If she resisted, the threats escalated. Sometimes the threats were directed at her; other times they involved threats to report her to immigration authorities.

Eventually she explains that she learned to comply quickly because doing so often prevented the violence from getting worse.

At that moment, the lawyer may begin to see the situation differently.

What the client experienced was not simply repeated sexual assault within a relationship. It was a pattern in which sexual acts were coerced through threats connected to something of value: her safety and stability.

Once you understand this dynamic, your legal analysis can shift toward trafficking.

For practitioners, these moments illustrate why consultations should go beyond surface descriptions of abuse. The legal framework of trafficking often becomes visible only when lawyers explore the mechanisms of control operating within the relationship.

When those mechanisms come into focus, cases that once appeared to be solely domestic violence cases may reveal an additional layer of exploitation that the trafficking laws were designed to address.

Business Exploitation and E-2 Investor Cases

Let's explore fact patterns involving lawful visa holders (such as a German E-2 investor) whose business partners use threats of visa cancellation, financial manipulation, and immigration leverage to force unpaid labor and control profits.

When a Business Partnership Becomes Coercion: E-2 Investors and Hidden Exploitation

Trafficking does not only occur in physically demanding industries like construction. Sometimes it appears in places where we expect to find business opportunity and entrepreneurship rather than exploitation. One example that surprises many practitioners involves investors or business partners who enter the United States through lawful visa programs, such as the E-2 treaty investor visa. Because these clients often have financial resources and entered the country legally, lawyers frequently misdiagnose their situations as standard breach of contract or business dispute cases.

On paper, these situations almost always begin as legitimate business arrangements. An investor from another country contributes capital to launch or expand a business in the United States. The investor may become actively involved in the day-to-day operations of the company, especially during the early stages when the business requires constant attention. The visa itself is intrinsically tied to the success and continuation of the enterprise, meaning the investor has a massive personal incentive to ensure the business survives.

However, that exact regulatory structure can create extreme vulnerability when a business partner or controlling party begins to misuse that immigration leverage. Unlike many traditional employment relationships, E-2 investors tie their immigration stability directly to the functioning of a specific business. If the enterprise collapses, the visa status generally collapses right along with it. A manipulative partner who understands this dynamic can easily weaponize it to exert control over the investor.

At first, the pressure usually appears subtle and looks like a typical business disagreement. The American partner might begin shifting more daily responsibilities onto the immigrant investor while simultaneously reducing their own involvement. Financial transparency slowly disappears, and the investor may find themselves working longer hours to keep the business operating while their partner controls the bank accounts. Over time, the dynamic transforms from an unequal partnership into a highly coercive environment where the investor has lost all autonomy.

The Hypothetical: The German E-2 Investor Trap

Imagine a German entrepreneur named Lukas who enters the United States on an E-2 visa to open a small manufacturing company in Ohio with an American partner. At first, the business partnership appears completely legitimate. Lukas invests significant capital, relocates his life, and works long hours building the company from the ground up. The initial agreement was that Lukas would manage daily operations while the U.S. partner handled the finances and long-term strategy.

Over time, however, the relationship begins to fundamentally change. The U.S. partner gradually stops participating in the business entirely but continues to aggressively withdraw money from company accounts for personal use. When Lukas realizes the business is suffering and asks for financial transparency, the partner becomes defensive and immediately threatens Lukas's immigration status. The partner explicitly tells Lukas that if he challenges the financial arrangements or tries to hire an outside accountant, the partner will shut down the business or legally withdraw from the partnership.

Because Lukas's immigration status depends entirely on the business remaining operational, these threats carry enormous, terrifying weight. Lukas finds himself working eighty hours a week, performing all the manual labor and management duties just to keep the doors open. He is not receiving his share of the profits, his capital investment is being stolen, and he cannot leave because doing so would mean losing both his livelihood and his legal ability to remain in the United States. The U.S. partner understands this power dynamic and uses it repeatedly to make Lukas to provide unpaid sweat equity.

For an immigration lawyer sitting across the desk from Lukas, recognizing that shift is absolutely crucial. The partner is using immigration leverage to control Lukas's labor and financial contributions, which squarely meets the definition of abuse of the legal process. Under the trafficking regulations, abuse or threatened abuse of the legal process is a recognized form of coercion. Because this coercion is being used to make Lukas to continue working under conditions from which he cannot realistically escape, the situation has crossed the line into involuntary servitude.

How to Screen for Business Exploitation

This kind of scenario illustrates an important principle that appears across many trafficking cases: the mechanism of coercion does not always involve physical confinement or violence. Sometimes the pressure comes from economic vulnerability combined with severe immigration leverage. When those forces combine to trap someone in an exploitative situation, the legal analysis should move beyond civil litigation and into humanitarian trafficking protections.

When a client describes severe problems within an E-2 business arrangement, or any employment-based visa situation (such as H-1B or L-1B) where a sponsor holds power, lawyers should explore the dynamics carefully. These specific screening questions can help you reveal whether coercion and involuntary servitude might be hiding beneath a messy business dispute:

1. Who actually controls the business finances and the bank accounts? Whose names are actually on the business / accounts? Has your partner ever given you reasons you cannot be on the accounts or told you scary stories about people on accounts?

2. Have you been able to see accurate financial records for the business, or are you locked out of them?

3. Has your partner ever threatened that the business would collapse, or your visa would be cancelled if you did not continue working?

4. Are you performing far more labor in the business than originally agreed upon without receiving your promised compensation?

5. Have you ever tried to step away from the business or change your role, and what exactly happened when you did?

6. Has your partner ever threatened immigration consequences or deportation if you raised concerns about finances or working conditions?

7. Do you feel free to leave the business; do you think they might have tried to make you feel like you had to stay; or do you feel leaving might hurt your ability to remain in the United States?

8. I want to ask a sensitive question about something that can happen in these business situations. Did this person ever make inappropriate sexual comments or expect any sexual contact?

These questions are not meant to convert ordinary business disputes into trafficking cases, because many business partnerships experience severe conflict without rising to the level of coercion. But when a partner actively uses immigration leverage as a weapon to force labor or maintain total control over a person's livelihood, the situation demands serious T visa legal analysis. By identifying these patterns, you can offer a lifeline to professionals who never imagined they could become victims of human trafficking.

> **Pro Tip:** If the investor has a spouse, you may want to interview that spouse as well. We have found the trafficker will often compel the spouse to do all kinds of work for free, treating them like they are property since the investor works with them. Maybe in the end, the spouse's case becomes the T-1 instead.

> **Pro Tip:** Assume you have a T-1 case with a T-2 derivative. If the T-1 spouse is minimizing victimization, ask if you can interview the other spouse separately (this assumes you have cleared conflicts). One spouse might just remember more harm the trafficker caused them than the other spouse. There are a lot of reasons someone might minimize victimization. A caring spouse might remember a lot of it and give you some insight into questions that may help the main T-1 applicant feel more comfortable disclosing. Also, sometimes the main victim may have some memory loss due to the victimization, so ask about medical issues and memory.

Sex Trafficking Involving Minors

Let's consider scenarios demonstrating grooming, the "false school promise," recruitment through family acquaintances, and the legal reality that force, fraud, or coercion are not required for commercial sex trafficking of anyone under 18.

When cases involve minors, the legal framework for human trafficking is different. We spend so much time in adult cases analyzing the intricate details of force, fraud, or coercion to prove our adult clients were victimized. But when the victim is or was a minor, the law recognizes the minor's inherent vulnerability and requires less to establish T visa eligibility. Trafficking cases involving minors frequently look deceptively ordinary, hiding behind the guise of family arrangements, romantic relationships, or simple teenage rebellion. Because young people rely on adults for their basic survival, they often do not recognize that they are being exploited, which makes our job as practitioners during the screening process absolutely critical.

Sex Trafficking Without Force, Fraud, or Coercion

One of the most important distinctions in trafficking law is how it treats the commercial sexual exploitation of children. Under the standard model for adult trafficking, you should prove that the prohibited action was carried out (or attempted) through the means of force, fraud, or coercion for the purpose of a commercial sex act. However, a minor under the age of eighteen who engages in a commercial sex act meets the definition of a victim of a severe form of trafficking in persons **without you having to show force, fraud, or coercion**. Also, even if there wasn't a sex act, but there was an attempt to get to that point — you may have T visa eligibility under *attempted* sex trafficking.

Why isn't force required for minor sex trafficking cases? Minors under the age of eighteen cannot legally consent to sexual acts according to the legal definition. Because a minor fundamentally lacks the capacity to consent, the law presumes that any commercial sex act does not require coercion since there is no "choice" to be made by the minor in terms of consenting to sex. You do not need to prove that the trafficker physically restrained the child, beat them, or threatened to deport their family in order to win the case. The mere fact that the minor was induced to engage in a commercial sex act is entirely sufficient to satisfy the trafficking definition. What if the child thought the trafficker loved them, or was a runaway, or later on married? They still could not have consented at the time, so it is sex trafficking. There is no such thing as a "child prostitute;" only a child sex trafficking victim.

An investigator with decades of FBI experience working on anti-trafficking taskforces told me they had never seen a sex trafficking case with a minor that did not have one or all of the elements of force, fraud or coercion. This is probably glaringly obvious to many, but just because it is not required does not mean it should be glossed over in the victim statement. Also, when screening a potential client, it is worth trying to get a good timeline to see whether their sex trafficking began as a minor. Ultimately, though, with the T visa filing, if you are filing for a victim who is not required to prove force, fraud or coercion, make that clear to USCIS to save them some work.

Understanding Grooming in Child Trafficking

Overt force is not required. Sex trafficking of minors under 18 years of age often begins with an insidious tactic known as grooming. Grooming is a psychological process where an abuser uses emotional tactics to gain a victim's trust, isolate them, and put them into a vulnerable situation for sexual abuse. Abusers may be strangers, but also may be family members, friends, or trusted figures within their community.

Grooming typically begins with the abuser giving the minor extra attention or special treatment that makes them feel uniquely valued. In our practice, we frequently see cases of abusers offering young people desirable things like vape pens, makeup, hair accessories, or taking them out for fast food meals. The abuser uses these gifts as romantic gestures to cross normal boundaries and to create psychological dependency. We also see cases of abusers looking for vulnerable young people and offering them something they desperately need, like a couch to sleep on for the night, to create dependency for basic needs like food and shelter. Once that dependency is locked in, the abuser begins seeking sexual acts in order for the minor to keep receiving those gifts, resources, or attention. The abuser will often enforce secrecy by telling the minor that no one will understand their special relationship, or by threatening to ruin the minor's reputation if they ever speak up.

Hypothetical: Ariel's Story

Let us look at a hypothetical scenario involving a twelve-year-old girl named Ariel to understand how grooming operates in the real world. Ariel lives in a crowded apartment where her undocumented parents work extremely long hours just to pay rent. A family acquaintance, an older man who frequently visits the apartment complex, begins bringing Ariel small treats, snacks, and eventually buys her a phone with fillable cards. He tells Ariel that she is incredibly mature for her age and makes her promise to keep the phone a secret from her stressed parents, isolating her from her primary support system.

Over the course of several months, the older man's behavior shifts from friendly gift-giving to manipulative demands. He tells Ariel that he will stop paying for the cell phone and will tell her parents she stole it unless she agrees to perform sexual acts for him. Ariel feels completely trapped because she relies on the phone for a sense of connection and is terrified of the shame that would fall on her family if the man lies to her parents. Years later, when Ariel is a young adult sitting in your office for a consultation, she might cry and tell you that she was not trafficked because she "willingly" did those things just to keep the phone. As her lawyer, you have the privilege of telling her that because she was under eighteen, the law recognizes that she could never consent, and her life or safety or even a cell phone can constitute the "thing of value" that makes it commercial sex trafficking.

This example is full of coercion, so let's take that out of the equation and see if it's still trafficking.

Ariel's Hypo — Revised to Eliminate Coercion

Ariel is 16. A man in the trailer park invites her over along with some friends, to his back yard. Ariel goes knowing he is related to one of her schoolmates. He offers the teenagers beer and a vape. Ariel tries the beer, she tries the vape pen, and everyone is laughing and having a good time. The next time Ariel is walking by the trailer, the guy says hey, come in my backyard, I have more beer. She goes by and this time, he says let's go through the front door because you can pick which beer you want this time. She goes in. He leads her to the bedroom, making it clear that the drinks and gifts come with a sexual expectation. He has offered her a thing of value in exchange for a sexual act she cannot legally consent to. This is trafficking (or attempted trafficking). No coercion required. You may have a T visa case.

Labor Trafficking and the Power Imbalance

While the rules for sex trafficking are strictly age-based, cases involving the *labor trafficking* of minors *do still require* you to prove force, fraud, or coercion. So why do I talk about labor trafficking in the chapter focused on sex trafficking? Because the way adjudicators should evaluate coercion for labor trafficking victims is vastly different when the victim is a child. It takes significantly less pressure for an adult to coerce a minor, especially when that adult is in an authoritative role over the youth. Children are wholly dependent on adults for their food, shelter, and survival. Simply the fact that a child is in the care of their trafficker means they are highly likely to do whatever their caregiver instructs them to do. The massive power imbalance between a vulnerable minor and a controlling adult makes threats of homelessness, isolation, or arrest incredibly coercive.

For example, throwing food or garbage at a child and having them do excessive chores has been the basis of a successful T visa case. Your biggest obstacle in proving a labor trafficking case for a child will not be the coercion element. It will involve helping the youth (who may be an adult by now) come to terms with what happened and determining which manner of reporting to law enforcement they feel safe and able to pursue (if any). Understanding the power imbalance is important to helping younger people talk about the labor they performed, since at the time of the trafficking they likely lacked any normal work experience to compare it with.

The "False School Promise" Tactic

One of the most common and heartbreaking methods traffickers use to recruit minors for forced labor is through educational fraud. This occurs when a trafficker approaches a child's parents in their home country and promises that if they send the child to the United States, the trafficker will enroll them in a good high school and provide them with a better future. The parents, who are usually living in poverty and desperately want to give their child opportunities they never had, agree to the arrangement. The minor travels to the United States filled with hope, only to discover upon arrival that the educational opportunities were a complete lie.

Hypo for Labor Trafficking of a Minor: Sam's Schooling Story

Consider a hypothetical involving a fifteen-year-old girl named Sam who lives in poverty abroad. A well-dressed family acquaintance visits Sam's parents and promises that if they allow Sam to travel back to the United States with her, she will enroll Sam in an excellent high school. Sam is a brilliant kid who taught herself to read early and dreams of studying in a big city, so she is thrilled about the opportunity. But the very moment Sam arrives at the acquaintance's house in the United States, the plans for school completely vanish.

Instead of going to high school, Sam is told she needs to "help out." She is made to be the full-time, live-in nanny for the acquaintance's three toddlers and the maid for the entire household. Sam sleeps on a small couch in the living room, receives low wages, and is entirely dependent on the trafficker for her meals. When Sam asks when she can go to school, the trafficker tells her that she owes a massive debt for her travel and that if she tries to run away, the police will arrest her because she is undocumented. Eventually as the children get older, Sam is less useful to her traffickers, so they fabricate a fight about how she eats too much and kick her out. Sam gets lucky and finds a new job after getting some help from a local church. Years later, Sam might still feel grateful she is in America and blessed that she found freedom, but the education she was promised was stolen from her.

This is a case of domestic servitude. The trafficker used fraud — the false promise of a high school education — to recruit and transport Sam to the United States. Because Sam was a minor, the power imbalance made the threats of arrest and the reality of her isolation extraordinarily coercive. The T Visa Policy Manual explicitly recognizes that creating a situation where a person believes they will face homelessness or banishment if they refuse to perform labor constitutes severe harm. The trafficker framed Sam's exploitation as just "helping out the family," but in reality, it was a calculated scheme of involuntary servitude.

In a case like this, we might also consider filing T-4 petitions for Sam's parents abroad, to bring them to the US, if there is still a danger of retaliation such as reputational harm against the family due to Sam's escape or due to her reporting to law enforcement. T-4 parent cases based on retaliation danger can be filed regardless of whether Sam is a minor or adult, and if the risk extends to siblings, those siblings (adults or minors) could also come as the T-6 derivatives in a T-4/T-6 combo case. The justice is not only the legalization of Sam's status, but also family reunification and providing opportunities to the entire family to reset.

Sam's Story — Additional Screening for Sex Trafficking Required

Assume all of the above facts, which established labor trafficking, and now ask 3 more questions:

1. During the time you were living with this family, did anyone try to touch you in a way that felt weird? Or, were others allowed to be in the home, like anyone who made you uncomfortable?

2. Sam, I know this is hard, but when you were in this situation, did anyone ever offer you anything for sex or something like that? Did anyone do anything creepy, weird, or sexual towards you?

3. Did someone ever send you sexual or nude photos while you were there?

You may end up with a commercial sex trafficking case and not just a labor trafficking case. Both can be included in the T visa victim declaration. Don't forget to ask the sex questions.

While the case hypo I presented was strong enough, in my opinion, to win a T visa case based solely on labor trafficking, if there were sex trafficking attempts or elements present, it can be presented to USCIS as a T visa case involving both sex and labor trafficking. In the work I've done with Requests for Evidence and appeals, I have seen USCIS, the Administrative Appeals Office, and federal courts, more easily grasp sex trafficking of minor concepts.

Screening for Sex Trafficking of a Minor in Practice

Recognizing these cases requires immigration lawyers to ask incredibly careful, trauma-informed questions during consultations. Minors often do not view themselves as trafficking victims because they were conditioned to trust the adults who exploited them. When you are screening someone who experienced instability during their youth, you should ask about gaps in their schooling and whether they were expected to perform excessive chores for the people housing them.

A note on the word "chores" because we do not want to minimize the reality of domestic servitude and labor trafficking: "Chores" implies a standard, normalized aspect of childhood development, which fails to capture the coercive, exploitative nature of forced labor. Yet, in at least one FOIA response, USCIS noted excessive chores as a reason for meeting the T visa/involuntary servitude requirements — so it is shorthand that can be useful when trying to speak plainly.

Did you ever ask those questions to your DACA clients? Do you see now where you may find space to?

You should ask if adults ever provided them with housing, transportation, or money when they were under eighteen, and if sexual acts were ever expected in return. You also need to ask if they ever felt like they had to do something because someone threatened to hurt them, threatened to shame them publicly, or threatened to kick them out onto the street. Actively listening to a young person's story helps uncover the trafficking framework that a minimal intake would miss. For example, if the potential client says, "no but..." and pauses — just take a moment to let them say what did happen. A yes or no answer rarely gets us to the full story, so give time for the conversation.

If you have DACA clients, you already have a relationship with them. You already know their entry date, their age at entry, and something about their journey here. That is a foundation most trafficking practitioners spend months trying to build from scratch.

Here are a few questions worth weaving into your next renewal consultation:

- "When you first came to the US, who were you living with, and how did that situation come about?"
- "Were there ever gaps in your schooling after you arrived? What was going on during that time?"
- "Was there ever a period where an adult outside your immediate family was providing you with housing, money, or rides — and did that ever come with any expectations you weren't comfortable with?"
- "Did anyone ever make you feel like you had to do something — anything — or they would put you out, report you, or tell people something embarrassing about you?"
- "Did any adult ever send you photos or messages that

felt sexual or inappropriate when you were young?"

You do not need to interrogate your client; you simply need to invite the disclosure. Most have never had a professional ask these questions, and some have been waiting years for the opportunity to answer them. You may keep renewing their DACA while pursuing T status if needed.

You may also find out some things which, at first, you wish you didn't know, like maybe the parents on their birth certificate are not their parents. Maybe this is the year you find out someone had them misrepresent their entry date. You can request a waiver of misrepresentation if needed, for the T visa case, related to cleaning up those DACA issues. If a person were disqualified from DACA based on the truth, then we may not renew DACA and instead would focus on the T visa case going forward to make proper disclosures on the I-192 waiver for the T-1.

Often DACA holders have pro se filing histories, meaning they did not use a lawyer and may not have kept copies of what was filed. Or, they may not know a parent or someone else filed a case for them that later ended with a removal order in their absence. A FOIA to USCIS, CBP, OBIM, and EOIR will help you ascertain more background information to do a cross-check before you submit the T visa application to USCIS. If you do find a surprise removal order, you may plan to file a motion to reopen and terminate proceedings if/when the T visa case is approved.

Spiritual and Cultural Coercion

Let's explore cases involving exploitation through religious authority, spiritual manipulation, community shaming, or occult/"black magic" threats to compel labor or silence victims.

Human trafficking does not always require physical locks, hidden safes, or armed guards to keep a person trapped. Sometimes the most effective restraints are psychological, based on distortions of deeply held religious beliefs, cultural expectations, or community standing. As immigration lawyers, we are heavily trained to look for physical violence, confiscated passports, or threats of deportation during our consultations. However, if we only keep the most obvious checklist in mind, we could miss cases where the trafficker uses spiritual manipulation, religious authority, or occult threats to compel labor or silence victims. When a trafficker leverages a victim's faith or cultural identity against them, the psychological pressure can be profoundly paralyzing.

The trafficking regulations define coercion to include any scheme, plan, or pattern intended to cause a person to believe that failure to perform an act would result in serious harm. The USCIS Policy Manual specifically instructs adjudicators to consider the victim's cultural background, physical and mental condition, age, and educational level when evaluating whether a threat constitutes serious harm. For a devout believer or someone from a tight-knit cultural community, the threat of divine punishment, demonic curses, or total excommunication is the ultimate serious harm. For the victim, spiritual excommunication or a supernatural curse carries psychological weight as coercive as a threat of physical violence.

Recognizing spiritual and cultural coercion from a faith or culture different from our own requires us to step outside our own worldview and truly listen to the client's lived experience. It may help to research more about the faith or culture of your potential client, to prepare better questions. Traffickers intentionally exploit the power dynamics inherent in religious institutions and traditional family structures to mask their abuse as "spiritual duty" or "cultural obligation". Let us look at specific hypotheticals that demonstrate how this type of coercion operates in the real world, and how you can make strong legal arguments for your clients.

Hypo 1: The "Brujeria" Trap (Labor Trafficking)

Meet Maicol, who came to the United States from Central America to work for his family. The expectation was that family would help him, but they exploited him and violated wage and hour laws. His trafficker, who practiced *brujeria* (witchcraft), performed a specific occult ritual in front of him and placed a curse on him, stating that if he ever tried to leave the business, he would suffer terrible harm. For your T visa client, who grew up in a culture where these spiritual practices were deeply feared and respected, this was not an empty threat. It was a terrifying reality based on his deeply held spiritual beliefs. He stayed working for a very long time due to this faith-based coercion. He was subjected to wage and hour violations and treated like a servant. On top of that, he faced banishment or shaming by the family, if he were to leave.

This is a clear case of labor trafficking with faith-based coercion. In this specific instance, the serious harm threatened was supernatural harm, but it functioned exactly the same as if the trafficker had threatened to beat him with a baseball bat. When drafting this T visa declaration, you should explain your client's cultural background, so the adjudicator understands exactly why the threat of *brujeria* was paralyzing to a reasonable person in his specific circumstances.

Hypo 2: The Youth Pastor and the Teenager (Attempted Trafficking and Labor Coercion)

Now let us look at how spiritual coercion intersects with the unique, complex vulnerabilities of the LGBTQIA+ community. Consider Joe, a sixteen-year-old from a very conservative, religious community. When his parents discovered he was gay, they kicked him out of the house. He was isolated, terrified, and housing-insecure, which are vulnerabilities that traffickers actively hunt for. A charismatic youth pastor from a neighboring church approached him, offering him a place to stay in the church and promising the unconditional love and acceptance of God.

Very quickly, the pastor's motives emerged. The pastor began demanding that Joe work long, unpaid hours cleaning the church facilities and doing off-site work. The pastor used spiritual guilt and the threat of exposure as his weapons. The pastor insisted the unpaid labor was necessary "penance" for his "sinful lifestyle," manipulating religious doctrine to justify the abuse. A trauma-informed eye clearly sees that this is the abuser's weaponized language.

Because Joe was a minor, the power imbalance was massive, and the threshold for demonstrating coercion is viewed through the lens of his extreme vulnerability. However, even if your T-1 client were an adult, the pastor's actions would squarely constitute labor trafficking. Traffickers routinely target LGBTQIA+ individuals and youth because they know the fear of reporting abuse to authorities, combined with family rejection, keeps victims silent and trapped.

For example, consider the "anything of value" concept, where we are often considering things like food or money as the thing of value that commercializes the sex act in a T visa case.

However, if, for example, a transgender client believed she had to have sex with her trafficker in order to avoid "being outed" to someone (or to everyone), that is a "thing of value" scenario. **The coercion is a threat of outing, but also, the thing of value offered is "not to out" the person [safety, privacy] if they engage in sex without consent.**

Consider the converse - a transgender client may have suffered trafficking where the abuser/trafficker said things like "If you really want me to call you my girlfriend then you will do [some type of sex act]." The thing of value offered here would be essentially treatment with dignity or a trafficker respecting her gender identity. The thing of value is often deeply connected to the threat of harm.

Organizations like Immigration Equality are excellent resources for learning more about immigration options and ways to help your LGBT+ clients. You don't have to know everything always, but you can spend time learning and that is part of what is so beautiful about the work that we do.

Hypo 3: The Arranged Marriage and In-Law Servitude (Labor Trafficking)

Cultural expectations and community shame can be explicitly weaponized in domestic settings to compel labor. Imagine Priya, a young woman from India who comes to Chicago through an arranged marriage. Upon arriving, her husband's family insists on a "religious marriage" ceremony at a local temple, but they deliberately refuse to legally register the marriage with the county. This calculated move leaves Priya feeling religiously bound to the family, while simultaneously stripping her of any actual legal rights in the eyes of the state.

Almost immediately after the ceremony, her in-laws take complete control of her existence. They force her to work twelve-hour overnight shifts at a gas station they own, seven days a week, and they confiscate every single paycheck she earns. When Priya gives birth to a daughter, the in-laws secretly arrange to send the child back to India against Priya's will, telling Priya she must focus entirely on working at the store to pay off the family's business loans. When Priya asks to stop working so she can get her daughter, her father-in-law uses intense cultural coercion to shut her down. He tells her that she is a disgraceful wife, that she owes them her labor, and that if she ever tries to leave, they will spread rumors in their home village that she is a prostitute.

Priya endures this for three years until one day, her abuser is arrested for drunk driving. She eventually comes to you for a consultation. Her victimization is labor trafficking disguised as family duty and traditional domestic roles. The in-laws used the threat of reputational destruction, the intense isolation of a cultural community, and the withholding of her child to compel her labor. When drafting Priya's case, you should focus heavily on the "Power and Control" dynamics, clearly explaining how the in-laws abused cultural norms to create an inescapable condition of servitude.

One important clarification before we move forward: Priya's case is not a trafficking case because she had an arranged marriage. Arranged marriages are practiced across many cultures and religions as a respected tradition, and the vast majority of them are entered into with genuine family involvement, mutual consideration, and care for both parties. The T visa hypo for Priya is about what happens when a marriage tradition is distorted, when cultural traditions are distorted, for the purpose of making someone an involuntary servant.

What makes Priya's situation trafficking is the confiscated wages, the stolen child, the forced labor, and the reputational threats designed to silence her.

Those same facts could appear in a love marriage just as easily, and in my practice, they absolutely have. American citizen spouses use similar control tactics against partners they claimed to love deeply, tailoring their coercion to what will work against the victim best.

The arranged marriage context matters only because it explains why Priya's arrival created immediate vulnerability — she was in a new country, with people she barely knew, inside a structure that made questioning authority feel culturally dangerous. That vulnerability existed regardless of how the marriage was arranged.

Focus on the coercion. That is where the case lives.

Hypo 4: The Overworked Church Volunteer (Labor Trafficking)

Volunteering your time at a church, mosque, temple, or other religious community center can be a beautiful and normal part of human life. Pastors and religious leaders are allowed to ask their congregations to tithe, volunteer in the nursery, or help set up chairs for a service. However, religious leaders should be exceedingly careful about the enormous power dynamics they hold over vulnerable people in their congregations.

When a pastor or religious figure begins leveraging their spiritual authority, combined with a congregant's immigration vulnerabilities, to extract unpaid labor, they cross a very dangerous line. What begins as a joyful offering of time can slowly mutate into a rigid demand for labor. When the person can no longer safely say "no" without facing severe spiritual, social, or immigration consequences, the situation has moved from volunteering into involuntary servitude.

Let us consider a hypothetical involving an undocumented woman named Belinda. She is deeply devoted to her Christian faith and finds an incredible sense of belonging at a local church after arriving in the United States. Initially, she volunteers to clean the sanctuary on Saturday mornings and occasionally helps organize church potlucks. She loves doing this because it connects her to her community and gives her a sense of purpose.

The pastor of the church soon realizes that Belinda is undocumented, lives alone, and is desperate to remain in the good graces of the congregation. Slowly, he begins demanding more of her time and labor. The pastor tells Belinda that God has given her a "special calling" to serve the church, and he assigns her to run the church's full-time daycare center without any salary. He makes her clean his personal residence and hand over a significant portion of the meager wages she earns from her evening house-cleaning jobs as a "mandatory offering." He tells her to buy, cook and sell food with all proceeds going to the church.

When Belinda becomes physically exhausted and tells the pastor she cannot keep up with the demands, he weaponizes his spiritual authority against her. He says she is rebelling against God. Belinda feels completely trapped, terrified of divine punishment, so she continues to work for free.

The T Visa Policy Manual explicitly recognizes that compelled labor or services might include non-traditional types of work, and that perpetrators can use psychological abuse to establish coercion. Here, the pastor used a combination of fraud (manipulating religious doctrine for financial gain) and coercion (threats of spiritual banishment or spiritual harm) to force her to perform labor.

The concept of "serious harm" in trafficking law is broad enough to cover exactly what Belinda experienced. The statute defines serious harm as any harm — whether physical or nonphysical, including psychological, financial, or reputational harm — that is sufficiently serious to compel a reasonable person to continue performing labor. For an isolated, deeply religious immigrant woman, the threat of being excommunicated constitutes profound serious harm. The pastor used that fear to place Belinda into a condition of peonage and involuntary servitude.

Screening for the Exploitation of Volunteers

When you are conducting a consultation with an immigrant client, they will almost never describe their church or their pastor as a trafficker. They will usually defend the institution, believing that their exhaustion and exploitation were simply the heavy price of their own spiritual shortcomings. Your job as the attorney is to tactfully probe their volunteer work and examine the underlying power dynamics.

You can uncover these hidden cases by asking thoughtful, open-ended screening questions about their community involvement. You might ask: "Did a religious leader ever ask you to work for their business or church? What did they ask for? Did they ever talk about the punishment of God? How?"

You could also ask: "Did anyone at the temple (mandir) ever name you in front of others in some way that made you feel badly? Was it ever connected to doing more volunteer work? What type of services did you volunteer there?"

You should explore the financial dynamics by asking: "Were you ever asked to turn over your outside paychecks to a spiritual leader in exchange for their protection or blessing?" When you ask these questions, you can gently validate the client's experience while flagging markers of manipulation. You may gather the factual elements you need to demonstrate the force, fraud, or coercion required to build a successful humanitarian T visa case.

The survivor may blame themselves, believing they are fulfilling their spiritual duty or suffering the righteous consequences of their own sins. During your consultations, you should ask careful, open-ended questions about the power dynamics within their community and their religious circles.

You might ask: "What was the main reason you left this [religious organization]?" Or, "Were you ever threatened with public shaming, or being cut off from your religious community, if you did not do what they asked?" You could ask if the abuser ever claimed that God, the universe, or a spiritual curse would punish them if they stopped participating.

> Even if you are a business immigration attorney, screening for volunteer and faith-based trafficking could be a part of your intake; standard employment-based questions won't catch the T visa. Have you ever asked your H-1B clients about spiritual coercion?

When you take these cultural and spiritual threats seriously, and translate them into the statutory language of coercion, you can uncover the invisible forces that hold so many survivors captive. You give your clients the validation they may need to leave, and you build a compelling T visa case that adjudicators can truly understand.

Screening Exercises

By this point in the chapter, you've seen how spiritual and religious coercion operates across multiple case types — from Maicol's brujeria threats, to Belinda's unpaid church labor, to Priya's in-law exploitation dressed up as cultural duty. What ties all of these cases together is that the coercion is invisible to outsiders and often invisible to the client themselves.

You can find online several power and control wheels that describe mechanisms of spiritual and religious abuse. In this next lawyer's exercise, I have tried to adapt some of those concepts into screening questions. These aren't questions you fire off rapidly. They're conversation anchors. Use one, let it breathe, follow where the client takes you.

Below each question, I've left space for you to work through it as a practitioner. Think about how a potential client might receive that question. Ask yourself the questions as though you are the potential client. What defenses might go up? What language might you need to adjust? What does a "yes" look like when someone is too afraid to say yes directly? Remember, faith-based coercion is a distortion of religion or culture. It is not an attack on religion or culture, but it's a delicate topic.

1. Did anyone ever use your religion or your culture to tell you that you were required to obey them, even when what they were asking felt wrong to you?

How might a client react? How might you rephrase this in your own voice?

1.

2.

Note: Clients from communities with strong hierarchical religious structures may genuinely believe obedience was their obligation. They may answer "no" because to them, the authority felt legitimate. Listen for phrases like "he was my elder" or "it is our custom" or "I did not want to bring shame."

2. Did anyone ever tell you that if you left, or spoke up, or asked for help, God would punish you, or that you would lose your place in your community or your faith?

How might a client react? How might you rephrase this in your own voice to be a better screening question?

1.

2.

Note: This question goes directly to victim-blaming through scripture. A client may not connect the dots between religious language and legal coercion. They may describe feeling "spiritually unworthy" without identifying that someone engineered that feeling to keep them compliant.

3. Were you ever prevented from attending your own religious services, or were you told to attend a different congregation — one where you didn't know anyone?

How might a client react? How might you rephrase this in your own voice?

1.

2.

Note: Isolation through congregation-shifting is a trafficking tool. A client may describe this as a family decision or frame it as their spouse's preference. Ask follow-up questions about whether they had any friends at the new congregation, and whether anyone from their original community knew where they'd gone.

4. Did anyone from your church, mosque, temple, or community — a pastor, an imam, an elder, a family friend — contact you on behalf of the person who was hurting you, and pressure you to stay, forgive, or stay silent?

How might a client react? How might you rephrase this in your own voice?

1.

2.

Note: Community coercion is powerful precisely because it comes from trusted voices. A client may not recognize this as pressure — they may describe it as “people being concerned” or “everyone telling me to keep the family together.” The legal question is whether that collective pressure was used to maintain control.

5. Were you ever told that your medical care, or your children's medical care, was against God's will — and that seeking it would mean you were sinful or faithless?

How might a client react? How might you rephrase this in your own voice?

1.

2.

Note: Restricted medical care is both a trafficking indicator and a serious harm factor. A client who developed untreated injuries, chronic illness, or untreated mental health conditions because of religious restriction on care may have a compelling physical presence argument if that care is ongoing in the United States.

6. Were you married according to your religion, before you were 18?

How might a client react?

1.

2.

Note: Remember coercion is not required for commercial sex trafficking of a minor. Minors under 18 cannot consent, so no coercion required. This question is more related to a conversation about what might have commercialized a sex act — like an offer of staying in good with the church.

7. Did anyone ever use your faith to make you feel like you needed to participate in sexual acts you did not want? Or tell you that refusing was a sin?

How might a client react to these questions? How might you rephrase this question depending on the person's faith, educational level, or culture? How could you break apart or soften this question? While the T visa petition may refer to sexual acts, a client may use words like "go to bed with" or "make a baby" or "grow a family." We don't want to mischaracterize the abuse/reproductive coercion in screening, but we also need to be able to discuss the topic without alienating someone. While the future T visa victim declaration may refer to sexual acts, that is different from screening. You may need to use softer phrasing to start the conversation. At some point, you may need to be very direct.

1.

2.

Note: This is one of the hardest questions to ask and one of the hardest for clients to answer.

These questions don't follow a script. They follow the client. Your job in a screening consultation isn't to collect a checklist — it's to create enough safety that the truth has somewhere to land.

Every case in this chapter started the same way: someone had a case for a T visa but did not know it until the attorney identified it through the legal framework available. A debt that wasn't really a debt. A pastor who wasn't really a pastor. A husband who wasn't really a partner. A family obligation that wasn't really a choice.

Your job isn't to hand them the words nor exaggerate. It is to create enough space that they find their own way of explaining what they went through. With time and with more T visa education nationally, more people may initiate the consultation explaining what they went through and asking if it qualifies them for a T visa. For the most part, though, unless attorneys actively ask or educate the public and participate in extensive community outreach, it will be in the consultation where a person is likely informed for the first time that they appear to be a victim of trafficking.

The T Visa Policy Manual notes that USCIS adjudicators will consider "current efforts the applicant is undertaking to rehabilitate and stabilize, including self-identification as a victim or survivor," when evaluating whether an applicant's continuing presence in the United States is directly related to the original trafficking in persons. As a result, the screening and identification (or self-identification) of a victim or survivor plays an important role in the overall case.

The scenarios we've worked through here — the E-2 investor trapped by his business partner, the twelve-year-old receiving "gifts," the woman whose church became her cage — these aren't edge cases. They're the cases hiding inside your current caseload right now, waiting for a lawyer who knows how to look.

In Chapter 6, we turn from identification to execution. You've learned to spot the case. Now we need to talk about inadmissibility issues and the I-192 waiver, which is the real power of the T visa case: a broad level of forgiveness in exchange for honesty.

6

THE POWER OF THE T VISA WAIVER (I-192)

In this chapter we cover:

- **Requesting waivers for immigration/criminal violations.** How the T visa waiver (Form I-192) can cure almost anything, including criminal histories and immigration violations like the 212(a)(9)(C) so-called "permanent bar."
- **False Claims to U.S. Citizenship:** Using the T visa to overcome one of the most fatal immigration bars.
- **How to properly frame inadmissibility issues:** Discussion of inadmissibility issues, disclosure strategies, and potential client concerns.

Every immigration lawyer recognizes that feeling when a standard consultation suddenly takes a turn. You are sitting across from a potential client, sketching out a solid plan for a family-based petition, when they reveal that they were deported twice and came back across the border each time. Or they confide in you that their boss told them to check the "U.S. Citizen" box on an I-9 form ten years ago. Or they reveal a criminal record that includes multiple drug possession charges from a decade ago. They may be feeling terrible, having been told by others that there is no chance.

In standard immigration practice, these revelations often mean lifetime or long-term bars with no realistic waivers available. Early in my immigration law career, I had to deliver the heartbreaking news a lot. As I realized more and more family-based or employment-based cases with fatal flaws were related to victimization and started learning more about humanitarian waivers (T/U/VAWA practice), I discovered more doors were open to clients than I had previously believed.

The T visa waiver, filed on Form I-192 (Application for Advance Permission to Enter as a Nonimmigrant), operates almost like an eraser for inadmissibility. It is one of the most generous and expansive waivers created by Congress. It was designed with the clear understanding that human trafficking is a messy, chaotic, and destructive crime that often forces victims into situations where they break the law to survive. If we are going to protect trafficking survivors, we have to possess a legal mechanism robust enough to forgive the collateral damage of their victimization.

The Legal Framework of the T Visa (I-192) Waiver

To utilize the I-192 waiver effectively, lawyers use the two distinct statutory vehicles which give USCIS the authority to forgive inadmissibility.

The first vehicle is found under section 212(d)(13) of the Immigration and Nationality Act (INA). Under this section, USCIS has the discretion to waive applicable grounds of inadmissibility if the applicant establishes that the activities rendering them inadmissible were caused by, or were incident to, their severe form of trafficking in persons. For this, show a connection between the victimization and the ground of inadmissibility. In some of our CLE classes, attorneys ask if the trafficking MUST be connected to the ground of inadmissibility in order to win an I-192 waiver for a T visa case, and the answer is: No, it does not. However, if the trafficking was connected to a ground of inadmissibility, this gives USCIS the opportunity to waive it (forgive it) under section **212(d)(13)**. If the trafficking was not connected to a ground of inadmissibility your client needs waived, you may prevail under the second statutory vehicle.

The second statutory vehicle is also very broad. Under INA section **212(d)(3)** (also referred to as a *Hranka* waiver), USCIS has the general discretionary authority to waive most grounds of inadmissibility simply if it determines that granting the I-192 waiver is in the national interest. This means that even if a client's criminal conviction or immigration violation had absolutely nothing to do with their trafficking experience, you can still ask the government to forgive it. You will want to demonstrate that your client is a rehabilitated, contributing member of society, and that forgiving their past criminal or immigration violations serves the broader national interest of the United States.

For violent or dangerous crimes, you can explain extraordinary circumstances as well as any connection to the trafficking victimization, and you will also want to go deeply into hardship. That said, trafficking cases are often so severe and sympathetic, and a person's errors are often so connected to that experience, that we normally see USCIS apply favorable discretion in T visa cases.

You can find a section from the USCIS T Visa Policy Manual on the I-192 waiver, here:

https://www.uscis.gov/policy-manual/volume-9-part-o-chapte r-2 (Waivers for Victims of Trafficking).

"If an applicant is subject to one or more grounds of inadmissibility, the applicant may apply for a discretionary waiver of the ground(s) by filing an Application for Advance Permission to Enter as a Nonimmigrant (Form I-192). If the applicable standard is met and a favorable exercise of discretion is warranted, USCIS may waive all inadmissibility grounds for applicants for T nonimmigrant status under either INA 212(d)(3)(A)(ii) or INA 212(d)(13), except:

- Espionage or sabotage – INA 212(a)(3)(A)(i)(I);
- Any other security-related unlawful activity – INA 212(a)(3)(A)(ii);
- Overthrow of the U.S. government – INA 212(a)(3)(A)(iii);
- Adverse foreign policy impact – INA 212(a)(3)(C); and
- Participants in Nazi persecution or genocide – INA 212(a)(3)(E)(i)-(ii)."

As you can see, there are some grounds (like being a Nazi or a spy) that the T visa (I-192) waiver cannot cure, but those issues are extremely rare and have not come up in my practice.

For T visa cases, most grounds of inadmissibility — from fraud and smuggling to unlawful presence and criminal convictions — are theoretically on the table for forgiveness with the I-192 waiver. That is wonderful.

Additionally, the law explicitly exempts T visa applicants from the public charge ground of inadmissibility entirely, meaning you do not even need to file a waiver for public charge issues. In consultations, when I am explaining the TVAP program and wanting our client to accept the help they very much need, potential clients often ask if they will get in trouble for receiving help. It is so ingrained in culture that immigrants are not allowed to have any benefits that trafficking victims may be afraid to receive TVAP help. Explaining that T visa applicants are not subject to the public charge rules and that obtaining TVAP assistance is not something that will hurt their case, but rather help it, is important.

Another positive thing: since 2024, the USCIS filing fee for the I-192 waiver, if connected to a T visa case, is no longer required.

Curing the Permanent Bar

One of the most terrifying concepts in standard family-based immigration is the so-called "permanent bar" under INA 212(a)(9)(C). This bar is triggered when an individual accrues more than one year of unlawful presence in the United States and subsequently enters or attempts to reenter the country without being admitted. A permanent bar also can be triggered by re-entering or trying to re enter the U.S. after being removed (i.e., after being deported). Some law offices screen for the permanent bar by phone before a person even books a consultation and will reject booking the consultation! I do not do this.

In the regular immigration world, this bar requires the person to remain outside the United States for ten full years before they can even ask permission to apply for a waiver. It is a devastating penalty that separates families for a decade. I understand why some law offices don't want to deal with it and why they label it "permanent." I understand why being subject to this bar is deeply painful for clients and how awful it must feel to be told they have no legal option.

However, in the T visa context, the "permanent bar" loses its fatal sting. Because the I-192 waiver exists, a T visa applicant can request a waiver of the permanent bar on Form I-192 without ever having to depart the United States. This is an incredibly powerful tool for practitioners who are screening clients with complicated border histories. When you encounter a client with a "permanent bar," your immediate instinct should be to screen them meticulously for trafficking indicators, because a successful T visa application can completely neutralize this obstacle.

Consider a hypothetical consultation with a worker who was deported (removed) in 2015, only to return a month later by crossing the desert because his family was starving. Under normal circumstances, his unauthorized return triggers the permanent bar. But he tells you during the consultation that upon his return, he worked in a restaurant where his manager kept docking his wages by two hours per day, saying he was lucky he wasn't getting deported again. You can file the T visa petition alongside the I-192 waiver, explaining the circumstances of his entries and asking USCIS to waive the 212(a)(9)(C) inadmissibility along with other grounds of inadmissibility that he has triggered.

I still explain the "permanent bar" to potential clients and how we will disclose it on the I-192, so they are aware I am not missing something important that they may have consulted with other attorneys about. I go over how there is a difference between family and employment sponsorship rules, versus humanitarian ones. I explain that the name "permanent bar" overstates what this ground of inadmissibility is, and that it is a bar that can be waived with the T visa application. The "permanent bar" truly can seem daunting to practitioners and clients alike, but remember that this bar can be waived along with other grounds of inadmissibility in a T visa case, and that USCIS should also take into account whether there was any connection between the violation and the victimization. Even if the bar is not connected to the victimization, it can and should be waived generally on the I-192 for a T visa applicant who has suffered a severe form of trafficking.

The permanent bar should be taken seriously, but so should the broad waiver that you can seek to have it forgiven in the T visa context.

Waivers for False Claims to U.S. Citizenship

False claim to U.S. citizenship under INA 212(a)(6)(C)(ii) is widely considered an unforgivable penalty of immigration law. If a foreign national falsely represents themselves as a citizen of the United States for any purpose or benefit under the INA or any other federal or state law, they are permanently inadmissible. In almost all other areas of immigration practice, there is no waiver available for a false claim made after September 30, 1996. I have heard so many clients tell me they were told to give up hope the moment an I-9 form with the "U.S. Citizen" box checked becomes known.

The T visa/I-192 waiver is a game changer. Because the I-192 waiver for T visas is so expansive it includes the authority to waive a false claim to U.S. citizenship for a trafficking survivor, and as we have seen, a T visa can be processed faster than a U visa currently. This is monumental for your practice and for your clients' lives.

Employers might instruct vulnerable, undocumented workers to buy fake birth certificates or check the citizenship box on employment forms just to secure a job. The employers know exactly what they are doing, utilizing this federal violation as a tool of ultimate leverage. Once the worker has this problem, it is even easier for employers to exploit them. But, the false claim to U.S. citizenship can be waived under "(d)(3)" and "(d)(13)" — i.e., whether it is unrelated to the trafficking, or related to the trafficking. All on one form: the I-192.

> **Pro Insight:** See how what seemed like a major flaw (the use of U.S. citizen documents) ended up being a flag for trafficking?

Exercise: Can you think of any current or former clients with a false claim to U.S. citizenship problem whom you may want to call?

When you uncover a trafficking narrative involving an employer who used threats of deportation or economic control to keep a worker trapped, that worker's previous false claim to citizenship no longer has to be a life sentence of undocumented status. You prepare the I-192 waiver form, explicitly acknowledging the INA 212(a)(6)(C)(ii) violation. You explain the context in which the false claim was made, highlighting the client's vulnerability and other relevant factors, and argue that granting the waiver serves the national interest by protecting victims of severe exploitation. This is how you take a legally "dead" case and revive it.

Navigating Criminal Histories

Trafficking survivors are frequently forced into criminal activity by their abusers, or they resort to survival crimes due to the profound instability of their lives. A T visa applicant may have a record that includes sex work charges, drug possession, theft, or driving under the influence. When approaching these cases, lawyers should aggressively advocate for their clients without compromising candor to the USCIS adjudicator.

The 2024 regulatory updates provide clear guidance on how USCIS evaluates criminal inadmissibility. When exercising its discretion, USCIS will consider the number and seriousness of the criminal offenses and convictions that render an applicant inadmissible. Overall, I have found USCIS to be very forgiving of criminal history, and while it doesn't have to be connected to the trafficking to be forgiven, it helps if one explains any truthful connection to it.

There is also a highly effective practitioner strategy you should employ when the inadmissibility itself is legally questionable. Sometimes a client was arrested but never actually convicted, or they participated in a rehabilitative program that does not meet the strict immigration definition of a conviction. In these instances, you can use the "No, but if so, forgive" strategy outlined in the next paragraph.

On the I-192 form, you may argue that the client is not actually inadmissible under the statute because a formal conviction does not exist. However, you immediately follow up by stating that if USCIS disagrees and finds the applicant inadmissible, you are affirmatively requesting a waiver of that ground in the national interest. This protects your primary legal argument while providing a strong fallback position, making it easier for USCIS to approve a T visa case. Often, this is a short explanation on an I-192 addendum, and not a detailed "waiver affidavit" nor attorney brief.

Matter of M— and What It Teaches Us About Coercion and I-192 Waivers

There is a 1956 BIA case that predates T visas, but it's one of the best cases my original T visa mentor shared with me. The "Matter of M—" case refers to a 1956 Board of Immigration Appeals (BIA) decision (*Matter of M--, 7 I. & N. Dec. 251*).

Here is the short version: A Mexican woman was lured from her waitressing job with promises of better wages, trafficked in a "brothel" or "bawdy house," told she owed a debt she could never repay, and forced into prostitution until she escaped through marriage. The government tried to deport her for having engaged in prostitution. The Board said no — coerced conduct under duress is not, as a matter of law, the kind of voluntary prostitution that triggers deportability (and also noted she was not excludable as a prostitute).

The Board did not reach for discretion. They did not say "we feel bad for her, so we'll let her stay." They said the charge was simply not sustained because her conduct was not voluntary. They explained she was not legally responsible for acts committed while her free will was obliterated by wrongful threats and debt bondage, noting, "As a matter of law, she is not excludable as a prostitute under section 212 (a) (12) of the Immigration and Nationality Act of 1952, because *those to whom respondent was indebted reduced her to such a state of mind that she was actually prevented from exercising her free will through the use of wrongful, oppressive threats or unlawful means.* We have had occasion in the past to consider facts similar to those presented in the instant case and have held that prostitution committed under duress would not support a charge laid under section 241 (a) (1) of the INA. Accordingly, we find the charge stated in the warrant of arrest not sustained. The proceedings will be terminated." (emphasis added)

Now apply that principle to your modern T visa client's I-192 waiver form.

When your client has a sex work arrest, or drug charges connected to their trafficking situation, or even a false claim to citizenship that an abusive employer engineered, your first argument does not have to be simply "please waive this." Your first argument can be: *this does not constitute inadmissibility at all, because the conduct was coerced.* Matter of M— is your anchor. Conduct committed under the kind of duress that defines trafficking — fraud, coercion, debt bondage, threats — lacks the element of free will that underlies the inadmissibility grounds Congress was targeting.

Then, in the very next breath, you add the safety net to form I-192: but if USCIS disagrees and finds this conduct does trigger inadmissibility, we affirmatively request a waiver under INA 212(d)(13) and 212(d)(3), given its direct connection to the trafficking victimization and the national interest in protecting survivors.

That is your one-two combination. Lead with the legal argument that no inadmissibility exists. Follow immediately with the waiver request in the alternative. You protect the legal position and your client simultaneously.

Another option is for the client to accept responsibility for the crime or ground of inadmissibility and seek that it be waived due to rehabilitation, hardship, etc. Yet, asking a survivor to "accept responsibility" for actions that may have been coerced, manipulated, or born out of desperate survival contradicts the legal and psychological understanding of trafficking. However, will USCIS adjudicators expect acceptance of responsibility and give more weight to acceptance of responsibility than the coercive factors surrounding the behavior? It is worth discussing with your client the case strategy of first arguing they are not inadmissible and secondly, acknowledging the conduct triggering the ground of inadmissibility.

Also, it is worth noting that a client who accepts responsibility in some way is not necessarily admitting sufficient facts to warrant a finding of guilt. You may find a middle ground on how to disclose.

Empowering Inadmissible Clients to Highlight Their Resilience

After spending hours recounting the trauma of their trafficking victimization for the main declaration, on another day you are asking them to work with you on recounting their arrests, their unlawful border crossings, their DUIs, and their use of fake documents. It is an incredibly vulnerable position and can feel overwhelming for the client.

You can validate their feelings, explaining that the U.S. government recognizes that good people sometimes make impossible choices to survive, and that we are all human.

If the background is serious enough to the point where you feel a separate Waiver Declaration or Affidavit should be added to the I-192 waiver application, you help structure their waiver statement as a testament to their resilience. You want the adjudicator to read about the crimes or the violations, but then immediately read about how the client has attended rehabilitation, supported their children, and actively sought therapy to heal from their trauma.

When you frame inadmissibility issues this way, you empower the client. You shift the narrative from a focus on their past to a focus on their incredible capacity for rehabilitation and growth. They are entirely worthy of this humanitarian relief, and asking for forgiveness is a legal mechanism, not a final judgment on their character. A beautifully written waiver statement balances accountability with evidence of a life moving in a positive, contributing direction. If you choose this path, please carefully cross check your draft statement with any criminal history documents in your file and with a FOIA to make sure that you are not accidentally creating new issues through discrepancies between the different documents and your carefully written statement.

That said, most cases we file do not have a separate I-192 waiver statement. The I-192 form lists the grounds of inadmissibility needing to be waived and forms I-914 and I-192 have questions related to inadmissibility where you can be sufficiently responsive.

If USCIS wants more information, they can mail an Request for Evidence (RFE) to the law firm and explain what exactly they want more information about. An RFE narrows down what concerns USCIS actually has and is an opportunity for us to respond to those specific concerns.

Filling Out the I-192: A Lawyer's Walkthrough

The I-192 form itself is not complicated. What makes it hard is the vulnerability it requires — from your client to disclose painful truths, and from you as their advocate to present them clearly.

The form asks you to list each ground of inadmissibility for which you are requesting a waiver. You do not get to be vague. You identify the specific INA section and describe the underlying facts briefly (often 1 or 2 sentences at most).

Here is an example of an answer to Question 26 on the Form I-192 for a hypothetical case:

Immigration and Criminal History

26. Explain the grounds of inadmissibility that may apply in your case.

Please waive the INA 212(a)(7)(B)(i)(II) (documentation requirements), INA 212(a)(7)(A)(i)(I) (inadequate documentation), INA 212(a)(6)(A)(i) (presence without admission or parole), INA(212(a)(6)(E)(i) (smugglers), and any other grounds of inadmissibility apparent from the application, supporting documents, statements, and background checks. See attached Addendum for more information.

Image: Sample answer to Question 26 of Form I-192.

The addendum briefly explains the facts that triggered inadmissibility.

Inadmissibility Quick Reference Sheet – INA 212:

This list does not include all of the inadmissibility grounds, just the ones that I have encountered most frequently in our T visa work. Here are some of the most common grounds of inadmissibility you will be asking USCIS to waive (forgive) on I-192 applications in T visa practice, along with a few comments or pointers:

INA 212(a)(1)(A)(iii): Mental or physical disorder that has or may pose a threat to self or others. For example, this can be triggered if client victim statement, therapy treatment statement, or psychological evaluation mentions suicidal ideation or multiple DWIs, without info showing rehabilitation. USCIS may issue an RFE and can request a medical exam (typically an I-693) if the client statement indicates suicidal or homicidal ideation. If you see that language come up, please ensure you are addressing it appropriately. Often the mental health provider will address it as something treated in the past or actively being treated. Many clients have trauma and have a diagnosis of depression, anxiety, adjustment disorder, or PTSD. That does not mean they cannot obtain a T visa. To the contrary, being treated for that is a positive step for the case as it shows they are receiving help as a trafficking survivor.

INA 212(a)(1)(A)(iv): Drug abuser or addict. We are not doctors or psychologists to make such an assessment, but sometimes if USCIS sees multiple DWIs or extensive drug use mentioned, they will RFE about this ground of inadmissibility and can request a medical exam (typically an I-693) along with supporting documentation from medical/mental health providers. We have seen cases where traffickers give drugs or alcohol to a person to get them addicted and to use that addiction against them as coercion for the purpose of either involuntary servitude or commercial sex trafficking. In other cases, traffickers targeted a victim who already had a problem with substance abuse. Remember to screen the circumstances around this ground of inadmissibility for trafficking flags.

INA 212(a)(2)(A)(i)(I): Conviction or admission of acts constituting essential elements of a **Crime Involving Moral Turpitude** – please flag if your client has a criminal conviction; additional "crimmigration" research will be needed for explanation on I-192 form. Petty offense and youthful offender exceptions may apply. Tip on shoplifting: it may be survival-based related to domestic-violence based trafficking. Crimmigration analysis is the evaluation of how criminal records and immigration laws interact, identifying exactly which offenses trigger inadmissibility and require formal forgiveness.

INA 212(a)(2)(A)(i)(II): Conviction or admission of acts constituting essential elements of a violation of law/reg involving a **controlled substance** (drugs). Note that some states' definitions of drugs are not "drugs" according to the federal definition. Also, the client may not know enough to say whether there were controlled substances given to them or in bags they were made to carry across the border. Drug conviction analysis is heavily fact dependent. Will need "crimmigration" analysis.

INA 212(a)(2)(B): Multiple criminal convictions if total sentences to confinement were 5+ years. Will need "crimmigration" analysis.

INA 212(a)(2)(C)(i): USCIS has reason to believe that the client is a **controlled substance trafficker.** No actual conviction is needed for this ground of inadmissibility. Watch out for facts in the client's statement/FOIA results that may refer to having sold drugs even if the person was never charged or convicted. Heavily fact-dependent and legal analysis needed.

INA 212(a)(2)(D)(i): coming to the U.S. to engage in prostitution or has engaged in **prostitution** within 10 years of application. Note that this is not "solicitation." Also, see Matter of M regarding forced commercial sex under duress/may argue not inadmissible.

INA 212(a)(6)(A)(i): presence in the U.S. without admission or parole (EWI/entry without inspection).

INA 212(a)(6)(B): failure to attend a removal proceeding, without reasonable cause. Screen for whether the client was being trafficked or had any other reasonable cause to fail to attend a removal proceeding. If there was reasonable cause to miss the hearing, you may explain that briefly on Form I-192. If later pursuing a motion to reopen and terminate removal proceedings based on an approved T visa, the motion may note reasonable cause to fail to attend removal proceedings that lines up with the I-192. It is not required to have these facts, but if you have them, it may be better to explain on I-192 that there was reasonable cause to miss court.

INA 212(a)(6)(C)(i): misrepresentation of a material fact for the purpose of gaining immigration benefits. Examples: using another person's foreign passport and visa to gain entry to the US; lying on a tourist or student visa application; filing false statements with USCIS for other immigration benefits; lying when entering the U.S. about purpose of entry.

INA 212(a)(6)(C)(ii): false claim that they are a U.S. Citizen for benefit under the INA, Federal, or state law. Example: Presenting U.S. citizen birth certificate and SSN to DMV to get a photo ID, then using that ID to work at a factory and completing E-Verify/I-9 paperwork with it. As always, screen for whether there were coercive circumstances related to triggering this ground.

INA 212(a)(6)(E)(i): smugglers — helping anyone (including their family members) enter the U.S. in violation of the law. Example: paying for a coyote to bring a child to the U.S. across the border without permission.

INA 212(a)(7)(B)(i)(II): documentation requirements for nonimmigrants. For example, they do not have a nonimmigrant visa at the time of submitting their application. Often listed for EWI clients/clients who entered without inspection.

INA 212(a)(9)(A)(i): previously ordered removed, and who seeks admission again (within certain ranges of time).

INA 212(a)(9)(B)(i)(I): (3-year unlawful presence bar)– this is triggered if they accrue over 180 days but less than 1 year of unlawful presence, then leave the US, then seek admission. *Please note that this bar and the following two grounds **only** come into play after a departure from the US. If a client merely entered the U.S. with a visa and overstayed, these grounds are not triggered.*

INA 212(a)(9)(B)(i)(II): (10-year unlawful presence bar) – this is triggered if they accrue one year or more of unlawful presence, then leave the US, and seek admission again. There are exceptions to (a)(9)(B)(i) (I) and (II): certain time does not count as unlawful presence, including time in the U.S. as a minor under eighteen.

INA 212 (a)(9)(C)(i): unlawful presence after previous immigration violations (also known as the "**permanent bar**" (but can be waived for T and U visas): (I): unlawful entry/attempt to reenter after 1 year of unlawful presence;

or (II): unlawful entry/attempt to reenter after having been ordered removed (under any provision of law).

Please do not try to waive unauthorized employment with an I-192. That is an adjustment bar at INA 245 and is not an independent inadmissibility ground.

Keep it organized. USCIS adjudicators read hundreds of these. A clean, structured presentation — ground identified, facts summarized, argument stated — respects their time and makes your case easier to approve.

There is a pretty long list of grounds of inadmissibility, so keep a copy of the INA section 212(a) handy so that you can strengthen your correct, specific statutory listing on the Form I-192. There are many resources from AILA and ILRC (Immigrant Legal Resource Center) and ASISTA on inadmissibility analysis you can learn from. Remember, do not admit a client is inadmissible without first making that determination; and do not cover up or omit inadmissibility grounds of which you are aware. If you miss grounds that you are aware of or not, they will come back to haunt your client at the adjustment of status (I-485/green card) stage and will likely become a problem then, where an amended/*nunc pro tunc* I-192 waiver or other action may be needed.

When completing forms review (i.e., going through the immigration forms line by line before signature) with the client, the client may disclose additional grounds of inadmissibility that you need to address by revising forms. When your client goes through victim statement review, you may realize that part of their victim statement discusses events that may have triggered grounds of inadmissibility. While inadmissibility does not need to be tied to the trafficking for the I-192 to be granted, if it was, note it on the I-192 form.

Lawyer Exercises for the I-192

Question 1. Your client, Maicol, worked without pay for a family who threatened him with brujeria curses if he tried to leave. He also crossed the border without inspection twice, using a smuggler, and the second time was after living in America for 2 years without immigration status. Which grounds of inadmissibility are most likely present in his case?

A. INA 212(a)(6)(A)(i) (EWI entry) only

B. INA 212(a)(9)(C) ("permanent bar") and INA 212(a)(6)(A)(i) (EWI)

C. INA 212(a)(6)(E)(i) (smuggling bar)

D. No grounds apply because he was trafficked.

Answer: B. Unauthorized entry after accruing over 365 days of unlawful presence (here, 2 years) triggered the permanent bar under 212(a)(9)(C) and entering without inspection triggered (a)(6)(A)(i). Include them on Form I-192.

Question 2. Priya was brought to the United States by her H-1B-visa-holding husband on an H-4 spousal (dependent) visa. He forced her into unpaid domestic labor and threatened to report her to immigration authorities if she complained. Priya's visa expired two years ago, and she remained in the US. After escaping her trafficking situation, she filed *pro se* for an I-539 extension of stay but lied on the application about her work history. The extension was denied. Which ground is most relevant for the T-1 case/I-192 waiver application?

A. INA 212(a)(9)(B) — ten-year bar for unlawful presence

B. INA 212(a)(2)(D) — prostitution

C. INA 212(a)(6)(C)(i) — misrepresentation

D. None, because she entered lawfully.

Answer: C. Priya entered lawfully but overstayed, accruing unlawful presence. The ten-year bar under 212(a)(9)(B) applies once she departs — but she has not departed. The misrepresentation ground of inadmissibility related to giving untruthful information on an I-539 extension should be noted on the I-192 form.

Question 3 (True or False). A T visa applicant must depart the United States and wait ten years before requesting a waiver of the permanent bar under INA Section 212(a)(9)(C).

Answer: False. This is the rule for standard family-based immigration petitions like a case based on marriage to a U.S. Citizen. In contrast, for T visas, the I-192 waiver allows T visa applicants to request a waiver of the permanent bar without departing the US. This is one of the most powerful distinctions between T visa practice and family-based practice.

Question 4 (True or False). If a client made a false claim to U.S. citizenship on an I-9 form at their employer's direction in 2026, there is no available waiver in immigration law.

Answer: False. In most immigration contexts, this is tragically true. However, the T visa I-192 waiver, if granted, will waive false claim to U.S. citizenship. When an employer instructs a vulnerable, undocumented worker to check the citizenship box — and uses that act as leverage to control them — that is both a trafficking indicator and a waivable ground. Connect the false claim to the coercive employment relationship. The I-192 waiver and T visa can be approved.

Hypothetical Client Conversations

These are conversation anchors, not scripts. Adapt them to your client's language, pace, and emotional state.

Scenario 1: The Client Who Doesn't Want to Disclose

You've identified that your client, Belinda, crossed the border without inspection and worked at a church without pay under threats of spiritual punishment. She is terrified about admitting the unauthorized crossing as well as the fake papers she used.

You: "Belinda, I need to talk with you about something that might feel scary, but I want you to understand why it's actually good news. The T visa application includes a form where we ask the government to forgive certain things in your past — things like crossing the border without papers and using a U.S. citizen's papers to work. We don't hide it. We tell them exactly what happened, and then we explain why."

Belinda: "Won't saying that get me deported?"

You: "If we don't disclose it, and they find out, that's a problem for both of us. I can't lie to USCIS. When we disclose it on the forms, we are making it easier for USCIS to approve your T visa case. The truth is that you came here because someone promised you a safe place, and instead they exploited you. That border crossing and unlawful presence is connected to your trafficking. We use that connection to ask for approval of the waiver. Even if this was not connected to the abuse, this can be forgiven with a T visa case. I cannot promise or guarantee a result in a case, but USCIS's regulation says that generally USCIS does not place a person into removal proceedings if a case is denied unless they are a terrorist, trafficker, or have a specific type of criminal history. [Note: you will need to discuss further with her what would happen if removal proceedings were started anyway; appeals/motion processes; and other concerns, in further detail, because her question is not just about disclosure, it is about what happens to pending or denied applications broadly].

Scenario 2: The Client with a Criminal Record

Your client Joe, exploited by a youth pastor, has a ten-year-old drug possession arrest. He pled guilty, completed probation, and has had no issues since.

You: "Joe, I see the 2014 arrest. I need you to walk me through that period of your life."

Joe: "I was using drugs back then. The pastor told me the drugs were a spiritual failing. I got clean, and my kids are doing well in school."

You: "That matters legally. The shame he created around that arrest — that's part of how he controlled you. When we file the I-192, we acknowledge the conviction honestly. Then we explain the context: you were isolated, manipulated, and that period of your life was shaped by his abuse. We also show who you are now. Ten years clean, employed, raising your kids. USCIS sees the whole person." Again, this conduct does not have to be connected to the trafficking, but when you have real conversations with clients, it might help them feel better about seeking the I-192 waiver for their T visa case.

The pattern across these exercises is the same. In T visa practice, disclosure is the foundation of the waiver argument. Your client's worst immigration moment is often your strongest evidence of how deeply the trafficking damaged their life — and how profoundly they deserve this relief.

Scenario 3: The Client Whose Criminal History Has Nothing to Do with the Trafficking

Sometimes the inadmissibility issue and the trafficking experience don't connect at all.

Meet Dani. She came to the United States on a tourist visa fifteen years ago, overstayed, and eventually built a quiet life cleaning offices at night. Eight years ago, long before any trafficking occurred, she was arrested for shoplifting — but it was an expensive item she took, and she ended up with a felony level conviction. Four years later, a labor recruiter placed her with a cleaning company whose owner withheld her wages for months, threatened to report her if she complained, and forced her to work double shifts at properties the agency never disclosed. Classic labor trafficking.

Assume for the sake of this hypo, that Dani's shoplifting conviction is a crime involving moral turpitude under INA 212(a)(2)(A)(i)(I). She has no argument (nor should she manufacture one) that the shoplifting was connected to the trafficking. It happened years earlier. The two are separate chapters of her life.

This is where INA 212(d)(3) and *Matter of Hranka* become your tools.

Hranka established a three-factor balancing test for discretionary nonimmigrant waivers: the risk of harm to society if the person is admitted, the seriousness of the prior violation, and the reasons for seeking entry. The BIA deliberately rejected any requirement of extreme hardship. The standard is forward-looking and equitable, not punitive. In that case, the BIA chose to allow a Canadian woman with a criminal conviction to come to the United States for the simple purpose of going on excursions and even dates. Our T clients' reasons for seeking entry, like Dani's, are so much more compelling than that.

Run Dani's facts through those three factors.

Risk of harm to society? Minimal. She committed a single theft offense and has had no issues since. Seriousness of the violation? Medium. No one was physically hurt, she paid later for the item she took, etc. Reasons for seeking admission? Substantial. She is a trafficking survivor cooperating with the government's interest in protecting victims and prosecuting exploitative employers. Congress passed the TVPA to extend protection to people in her situation.

Even under *Hranka* alone, this waiver should be granted. But in a T visa case, you go further. The T visa statutory scheme is a humanitarian, victim-centered framework. Your argument becomes layered: *even under the baseline discretionary standard, the equities favor Dani — and under the T visa framework, they are stronger still.*

I-192 Denials and Appeals/Motions to Reopen or Reconsider

I have been very fortunate in my law practice, but I have had to deal with denials just like any other immigration attorney with nearly 20 years in practice. A denial feels devastating but can be remedied.

If you receive a denial on an I-192, your next move may be the I-290B, a Notice of Appeal or Motion filed with the Administrative Appeals Office (AAO). In my experience, a well-constructed I-290B can absolutely turn a denial around, including in cases where a client has a felony drug history, embezzlement, or an assault conviction.

There is a collection of older BIA decisions that collectively stand for a powerful proposition: USCIS and immigration judges have repeatedly underestimated how much time, rehabilitation, and changed circumstances matter in I-192 adjudications, and they have been reversed on appeal.

1. *Matter of Ronald James Duffus*, A 096-127-539 (BIA Nov. 13, 2007) (denial of I-192 overturned for applicant who was previously convicted of sexual assault and driving under the influence sixteen years prior to the application filing date);

2. *Matter of Kenneth Lawrence Aiken*, A 099-001-692 (BIA Aug. 30, 2007) (denial of I-192 overturned for applicant who was convicted of assault with a deadly weapon);

3. *Matter of Peter Phillip Mahoney*, A070-517-063 (BIA Jan. 13, 2009) (denial of I-192 overturned for applicant who was convicted of conspiracy to traffic narcotics).

The above were not minor traffic violations. These are serious criminal histories, and the government consistently found that the equities, the rehabilitation, and the circumstances of the application outweighed the denial so that the I-192 could be approved. These were not T visa cases (Form I-192 is used in a handful of other cases), but they are helpful for T visa cases and Requests for Evidence Responses.

What this tells me, and what I tell colleagues who feel defeated after a denial, is that a first-level denial is not the final answer. Build your I-290B methodically, with evidence of rehabilitation, clear equities, and explicit engagement with the *Hranka* factors.

One clarification: everything I just walked you through — the 212(d)(13) trafficking-related inadmissibility argument, the 212(d)(3) *Hranka* argument — this is a lot. But you are not filing more than one I-192 for your T-1 client. You are filing one Form I-192 per client if there are inadmissibility grounds to be waived. You are not filing two separate waiver applications or writing two separate briefs for this T-1 case.

In the vast majority of T visa cases I handle, the I-192 itself does the heavy lifting. You identify the ground, state the relevant statutory authority, and write a concise explanation of the potential inadmissibility trigger. Most of the time, that is genuinely enough. USCIS adjudicators working T visa cases understand the humanitarian framework. They are not looking for a law review article. They are looking for honesty, clarity, and context.

Reserve the detailed waiver declaration for the situations that truly demand one — a violent felony, a multi-year drug trafficking conviction, something that will stop an adjudicator cold without substantial explanation. Even then, you are telling a human story of survival and rehabilitation, not writing an appellate brief.

The form is the vehicle. Your job is to present correct information cleanly and trust the framework Congress built for exactly these survivors. If the USCIS adjudicator still does not understand, prepare to take the case to the next administrative level.

As you improve your understanding of each potential ground of inadmissibility listed in the INA, you can also improve your understanding of the humanitarian reasons for waiving those grounds of inadmissibility. While each basis for winning the I-192 waiver has a different framework, the USCIS T Visa Policy Manual helps lay out some things you can focus on for (d)(13) (trafficking-related) versus (d)(3) (general *Hranka*) waivers.

For example:

For the (d)(13) waiver for trafficking-related grounds of inadmissibility, factors USCIS officers "may consider in determining whether a waiver is in the national interest include, but are not limited to:

- Details of the applicant's victimization;
- Level of victim's cooperation with law enforcement;
- Contributions to public safety by strengthening the ability of law enforcement to investigate and prosecute criminal activity;
- Contributions to the community;
- Family unity; and
- Risk of harm if returned to home country." (USCIS T Visa Policy Manual, Part O, Chapter 3).

To make a decision on the I-192, the USCIS adjudicator must "weigh the social and humanitarian considerations against the adverse factors present in the applicant's case. The approval of a waiver as a matter of discretion depends on whether the favorable factors in the applicant's case outweigh the unfavorable ones. In cases involving violent or dangerous crimes, USCIS only exercises favorable discretion in extraordinary circumstances, unless the criminal activities were caused by, or were incident to, the victimization that the applicant suffered as a result of being trafficked." (USCIS T Visa Policy Manual, Part O, Chapter 3).

Furthermore, if the USCIS adjudicating officer determines that the applicant is not eligible for a waiver under INA 212(d)(13) (i.e. the trafficking-related waiver), the USCIS officer *must* consider whether the applicant meets the legal standard and warrants a favorable exercise of discretion under the INA 212(d)(3)(A)(ii) nonimmigrant waiver. (You can find more citations and analysis in the USCIS T Visa Policy Manual section, Part O, Chapter 3). That refers us back to the general non-immigrant waiver (*Hranka).*

You don't need to memorize this now; you just need to know that you have at least two options to go through when preparing form I-192 or when responding to a Request for Evidence. USCIS officers sometimes forget one step or the other and only refer to one of the statutory vehicles under which the I-192 can be approved when they write and issue an RFE. If you get an RFE like that, you can help win a case by reminding the adjudicator of how your client meets one or both.

The I-192 waiver in removal proceedings. In light of *Loper Bright Enterprises v. Raimondo*, 603 U.S. 369 (2024), practitioners should consider whether the long-standing assumption that USCIS has exclusive authority to adjudicate Form I-192 inadmissibility waivers in the T visa context remains legally sound. Because *Loper Bright* eliminated Chevron deference, courts are now required to independently interpret the governing statutes and regulations rather than defer to an agency's interpretation of ambiguous provisions. This shift may support an argument that Immigration Judges possess jurisdiction to adjudicate Form I-192 waivers in removal proceedings involving T visa applicants, much as several circuit courts have recognized Immigration Judge authority over waivers in the U visa context. See *L.D.G. v. Holder*, 744 F.3d 1022 (7th Cir. 2014); *Baez-Sanchez v. Sessions*, 872 F.3d 854 (7th Cir. 2017); *Meridor v. U.S. Attorney General*, 891 F.3d 1302 (11th Cir. 2018); and *Jimenez-Rodriguez v. Garland*, 996 F.3d 190 (4th Cir. 2021). The post-*Loper Bright* framework provides a basis for arguing that the question of adjudicatory authority should be resolved through independent judicial interpretation of the Immigration and Nationality Act and its implementing regulations rather than by deference to agency practice.

7

Deportation Defense & Revisiting Denied Cases

In this chapter, we will cover use of the T visa in removal (dcportation) dcfcnsc, including:

- **Administrative closure** (of removal proceedings) for pending T visa cases, and continuances.
- **Mandatory Termination:** Enforcing the mandatory termination of removal proceedings once a T visa is approved.
- **ICE Deconfliction:** Using ICE's own memos to pause civil immigration enforcement while your victim-based application is pending.
- **Fighting NTAs:** Holding the agency accountable to 8 CFR 214.204(b)(3) if a T visa is denied.
- **Rescreening failed cases** of many types, for T eligibility (one of my favorite things to do).

When an immigration lawyer sees a Notice to Appear (NTA), the traditional instinct is to immediately shift into a purely defensive posture. We are trained to look at the immigration court system as a battlefield where the available weapons are asylum, cancellation of removal, or begging for prosecutorial discretion. But when you understand how to utilize the T visa framework, your entire approach to removal defense changes. The T visa is not just a humanitarian benefit. It provides mechanisms to pause civil immigration enforcement, stay final orders of removal, and ultimately trigger a regulation that requires the immigration judge to terminate proceedings completely, mandatorily.

If your client is in removal proceedings when you first meet them, the T visa process is available to them.

The T visa filing rules on "where to file the T visa if your client is in removal" are straightforward. Whether your client is the principal applicant or a derivative, and regardless of whether they are in removal proceedings, the T visa application goes directly to USCIS, not to the immigration judge. That means that the T visa application will be decided out of court, by USCIS, not the immigration judge. This means there generally is not an immigration "trial" in a T visa case, and USCIS should decide the case on paper, meaning a final decision is mailed to the immigration attorney (hopefully in the form of a T visa approval notice and work permit).

I will note there is a limited exception regarding immigration courts handling I-192 waiver decisions which we will not cover here as it goes into jurisdictional splits and other gymnastics. For the purpose of this chapter, we will focus on T visa cases where the decision is being made by USCIS, which is the agency where the T visa application gets filed and decided.

Now, what happens to the immigration court case while USCIS is working through the T visa application? We already know that the current processing time is 32+ months for T visa adjudication, and an immigration court hearing like a Master

Calendar or Individual Hearing might happen sooner than that.

We know that USCIS processing times are a mathematical mystery to some extent. USCIS's processing-time figure is not a true forecast. It is a backward-looking measure that appears to estimate how long it took to complete 80% of adjudicated cases in the prior six months. So, if the site is currently showing 32+ months for Form I-914 (T-1 applicants), that is an 80th-percentile historical completion measure, not a promise that a July 2026 filing will finish in 31 months. The processing timeline and goal posts keep moving, and that is how it is for just about every case type USCIS processes, not just T visas.

Administrative Closure

As the USCIS Policy Manual states, DHS has discretion to join your client in a joint motion to administratively close or terminate proceedings without prejudice while USCIS adjudicates the case. This is not automatic. It requires DHS to agree. Some ICE counsel offices are cooperative on this, particularly if your client has already received a bona fide determination and has deferred action and a work permit in hand. Others resist. Your mileage will vary by jurisdiction, by the individual ICE attorney, and prevailing enforcement climate.

If DHS agrees, you file the joint motion for administrative closure with the immigration judge or the BIA, whichever body currently has jurisdiction over the case. Administrative closure essentially puts the removal case on a shelf while USCIS adjudicates the T visa. It doesn't end the removal proceedings, but it stops the removal proceedings for a period of time (indefinitely) — hence the name "administrative closure."

Termination without prejudice is a cleaner option for ending removal proceedings when available, but either mechanism buys your client breathing room.

Also, for clients who already have another form of relief pending in removal court (e.g., asylum), they may not want termination nor admin closure — they may want to keep the removal case active while also waiting for T visa approval. There are a lot of options to discuss individually with clients.

For those who want unilateral administrative closure while the T visa is pending, a motion for administrative closure may explain that a pending T visa application can be adjudicated outside of court, meaning it will save time and resources for the immigration court. The judge may more easily grant administrative closure if a bonafide determination (BFD) has been issued, since removal of the client must be stayed (stopped) anyway with a BFD. Notifying the court of a bonafide determination also helps show that there is a potential favorable anticipated outcome, since T visa approval would resolve removability through status.

I have collaborated with many removal defense attorneys, and the feedback I often receive is that explaining things clearly to the immigration judge helps a lot. T visa cases are still rare, and don't come across a judge's desk very often. A good attorney will be prepared to offer lots of options to the judge (and to opposing counsel), for a potential administrative closure grant, and if that can't be given at the moment, then the judge may grant a continuance for full T visa adjudication.

I still saw a case where the judge would not give more time, nor admin closure, and instead ordered removal. While the removal order was on appeal to the BIA, the T visa approval came through, allowing for reopening and termination of removal proceedings.

Final Orders of Removal: Can You File a T Visa Case Anyway?

Sometimes a potential client already has a final order of removal before you ever identify them as a potential T visa client.

If your potential client already has a final order of removal, deportation, or exclusion when they come to you, you can still file the T visa case directly with USCIS. A final order doesn't close the door to T visa relief. What it does mean is that you have a client who could be physically removed from the country at any moment, and the filing of the T visa application does not automatically stop that from happening.

The T visa filing does not stay the removal order (but we will talk later about deconfliction!). USCIS receiving the T visa application does not stay the removal order. Often, the T visa application simply remains pending normally, and when a Bonafide Determination is issued, at that point, the client's removal order is finally stayed (stopped) officially while the case is pending with USCIS.

If there is interaction with ICE: You may request an administrative stay of removal from ICE. If ICE grants a stay and your client is in detention, that detention can be extended during the stay period while ICE technically waits for the T visa adjudication to resolve. This is a difficult situation for any client and requires close coordination with ICE counsel and, if necessary, a habeas petition (in federal court) to push back on prolonged detention. Also, a mandamus lawsuit (in federal court) may push forth a bonafide determination to stay the removal of your client.

The most powerful provision in this entire framework is what happens upon approval. A USCIS approval of a T visa application cancels any removal, deportation, or exclusion order issued by DHS (i.e., expedited removal orders) by operation of law as of the date of approval. For removal orders issued by an immigration judge or the BIA, you will need to file a motion to reopen and terminate proceedings to formally clean up the record.

If the T visa application is denied, any stay that ICE granted is lifted automatically. That's the pressure point. That's why the quality of the application matters so much.

Still, a T visa appeal and mandamus lawsuit may put additional pressure on ICE to hold on removal so that your client's T visa case can finally be approved.

Hypo: Nia from Jamaica in Removal Due to Marriage-based Case Denial

Let us imagine a consultation with a woman named Nia from Jamaica who comes into your office terrified because her marriage-based green card was just denied. USCIS has accused her of lacking sufficient evidence to prove a bona fide marriage, and she has been issued an NTA (notice to appear) placing her in removal proceedings. She assumes you are just going to help her fight the deportation in court based on the marriage, but as you ask your screening questions, a completely different narrative unfolds.

- Nia originally entered the United States on a K-1 fiancé visa, but she eventually confides in you that the visa was actually obtained with the intent to commit fraud. In trafficking scenarios, the "intent" often belongs to the recruiter or trafficker, who coaches the victim, so you ask more questions.

- A person from her community in Jamaica had recruited her, offering her a supposedly well-paying job at a hair braiding salon in the United States and setting her up with a cousin to act as the petitioner for the K-1 visa.

- Once Nia arrived in the United States, she was told she did not even have to live with the supposed husband. She started working at the salon while the green card case was filed.

- At the salon, Nia performed her craft of Jamaican twist braiding. As I understand it, this process involves meticulous hair sectioning and twisting, which requires immense skill, patience, and repetitive physical exertion. This job could have been a labor of love, but the business owner was having none of that.

- Because of the non-stop hours demanded by the salon owner, the physical strain became unbearable. Nia's hands suffered from severe, chronic pain.

- When Nia tried to complain about her excessive hours or the crippling pain in her hands, the salon owner used the fraudulent immigration filings as a weapon. The owner said her visa and papers would be canceled and constantly talked about how she should be grateful for this opportunity to have any job at all.

- Nia was absolutely terrified that the authorities would instantly lock her up.

Now that the marriage case has collapsed and she is in removal proceedings, what will be the relief in court she seeks? As a T visa lawyer, you recognize that this is a labor trafficking case involving profound coercion.

You may prepare a T-1 visa application with a Form I-192 waiver to request forgiveness for the K-1 visa fraud and misrepresentation. Because the fraud was orchestrated by the trafficker and used as the primary mechanism of her coercion, you can build a powerful argument that forgiving the violation serves the national interest. While waiting on her master calendar hearing date, you can file a motion for a continuance with the immigration judge to allow for the T visa adjudication. This alerts the court that USCIS has jurisdiction over the underlying relief, allowing you to advocate for a pause in the civil immigration enforcement.

Eventually, the wait pays off when USCIS reviews the initial evidence and issues a bona fide determination (BFD) letter. Under the modern regulations, a BFD provides the applicant with deferred action and triggers an automatic stay of removal, deportation, or exclusion. This means your client is legally protected from physical deportation while she waits for the final adjudication, and she can finally access a work permit independent of her trafficker. When the T visa is approved, you can file a motion to terminate the removal proceedings entirely, explaining that with an approved T status, such termination is mandatory. The judge is required to dismiss the case, completely freeing Nia from the threat of deportation and opening a pathway to adjustment of status.

ICE Memo/Deconfliction and Enforcement

If your client is in removal proceedings, you should know how to navigate the complex relationship between USCIS and Immigration and Customs Enforcement (ICE). You can use ICE's own memos to pause civil immigration enforcement while your victim-based application is pending.

When ICE encounters a noncitizen who is known to be a victim of a crime or who has a pending T visa application, their own directives require them to "deconflict" with other agencies to ensure they are not compromising an ongoing trafficking investigation. Because this inter-agency communication takes time, it often works well in your client's favor by appropriately pausing unnecessary aggressive enforcement efforts.

Have you ever heard of deconfliction? It's basically a rule saying if one agency is investigating something, the other agencies should check in to make sure they aren't disrupting someone's investigation. Deconfliction is a mandatory inter-agency protocol. It requires investigative bodies to coordinate before acting, ensuring a civil immigration arrest doesn't compromise a federal trafficking probe or derail an active criminal investigation by another agency. Like in the movies where the feds come in, take over a local police investigation, and step on some toes, deconfliction can take time to sort out among agents and agencies.

With that in mind, if your client feels safe and is ready to report the trafficking, engaging actively with law enforcement can initiate deconfliction protocols that help pause civil enforcement. This allows time for an investigation and gives your client breathing room in removal proceedings while waiting for their T visa to be approved. This is not a delay tactic. Reporting decisions are prioritized around clients' emotional readiness and physical safety, not utilized as leverage to stall removal proceedings. This is a justice and due process tactic — the client's victimization deserves to be investigated by the appropriate agencies, and deconfliction protocols are there to help the client remain in the U.S. while this is done, so that the government does not lose an important witness nor let a human trafficker profit by having victims deported.

Remember, once a BFD is issued, you may also wish to pursue administrative closure with the immigration court. If the T visa is approved, file for termination of proceedings. If there were other relief in court you were seeking, file for that too. While USCIS has jurisdiction over the T visa case (meaning it will generally be decided outside of court), the court might have other immigration relief to consider while you're waiting on a T visa decision.

Pending litigation to protect victims. In *Immigration Center for Women and Children (ICWC) v. Noem*, No. 2:25-cv-09848-AB-AS, 2026 WL 1455004 (C.D. Cal. May 20, 2026), the U.S. District Court for the Central District of California preliminarily certified three nationwide classes and granted in part a preliminary injunction blocking the implementation of 2025 DHS and ICE policies that subjected noncitizen survivors with pending VAWA, U visa, and T visa petitions to routine arrest, detention, and removal. The court temporarily restored prior DHS victim-centered enforcement policies, including the 2011 and 2021 guidance, recognizing that Congress created these humanitarian protections to encourage victims of domestic violence, human trafficking, and other serious crimes to cooperate with law enforcement without fear of deportation. As a result, eligible class members with pending survivor-based applications regained important protections against enforcement actions while the litigation remains pending, making *ICWC v. Noem* one of the most significant recent federal decisions protecting applicants for T visas and other survivor-based forms of immigration relief.

Will Filing a T Visa Result in Deportation?

One of the most common questions clients ask during a consultation is whether applying for a T visa will put a target on their back. You should use the modern regulations as a shield. A T visa denial does not automatically mean deportation. If you encounter a situation where USCIS denies a T visa and subsequently attempts to issue an NTA, you should hold the agency accountable to 8 CFR 214.204(b)(3). You will argue aggressively before the immigration judge for termination or administrative closure based on the fact that the agency violated its own protective regulations.

Here is the regulation:

"**Referral of applicants for removal proceedings.** USCIS generally will not refer an applicant for T nonimmigrant status for removal proceedings while the application is pending or following denial of the application, absent serious aggravating circumstances, such as the existence of an egregious criminal history, a threat to national security, or where the applicant is complicit in committing an act of trafficking."

If your client is not a terrorist or human trafficker, and does not have an egregious criminal history, USCIS should not refer them to removal proceedings simply because a T visa case is pending or denied. Under the Biden administration, we never received an NTA over a denied T visa case. In 2025, USCIS issued some NTAs for denied T visa cases, and made mistakes because the applicants didn't have any significant criminal history nor were they traffickers or terrorists. One situation was resolved when both the ICE attorney and the immigration judge agreed to terminate removal proceedings that USCIS had initiated after denying a T visa. The applicant had sued USCIS for a writ of mandamus to push forward the T visa appeal faster. Removal proceedings were terminated, and the T visa appeal was successful (in 2026).

With that in mind, it is really important to stay connected to trends in adjudication and removal defense strategies (more than we can cover in this book). Overall, here are some tips:

- Do not let one denial shadow your entire career. What didn't work at one point may work later. Fight for justice for your client. A legal strategy that failed under previous policy guidance may succeed upon refiling or appeal. Re-evaluate, adapt, and litigate.

- Prepare a high quality T visa case and timely RFE responses, if needed. The better your case the more likely you will get your client out of removal.

- Prepare to educate and advocate for your client. T visa rules are not well known, even within the immigration court system, and so when you know your stuff, you can do better in court.

Looking at ICE's 2025 Enforcement & Deconfliction Memo with an Eye to Protecting T visa Clients.

Treat this next section as a lengthy brainstorm, knowing that there is pending litigation to fully invalidate the 2025 ICE policy in 2026.

ICE enforcement policy changes. New administrations rescind prior directives and issue new ones; and courts can invalidate the ICE enforcement policies instituted by a President. What is procedurally available to you in a T visa removal defense case in 2026 may look completely different in 2028. The arguments I'm about to lay out are grounded in what we currently understand the 2025 ICE interim directive to require, but I have seen this landscape shift dramatically over the course of my career. I have watched protections appear, disappear, and reappear in different forms, sometimes within a single administration.

So here is my strong recommendation: stay connected to regular attorney trainings on removal defense, and then do what you think is right. No one has a crystal ball, and it is often the novel, creative, and best argument that wins the day.

That caveat also runs in the other direction. An argument that a judge or ICE counsel rejected two years ago may land differently today. The judge's patience with a particular government position might have worn thin and you will be there in the right moment to show the judge a way to rule in your client's favor. Litigation is not static, and neither is the human element inside it.

With all of that said, let's talk about what this memo actually gives us to work with.

The Procedural Gap Is the Opening

The 2025 ICE interim directive (which is currently being challenged in court as unlawful and unconstitutional under *ICWC v. Noem*) represents an enforcement-first posture that many practitioners, myself included, find deeply troubling from a victim-centered perspective. The 2025 Trump Administrative ICE memo attempted to walk back affirmative protections that had developed over years of advocacy and litigation. The government's position is, essentially, that prior victim-centered guidance was discretionary and is now being replaced with a different discretionary framework.

But here is the thing about procedural requirements: they do not disappear just because the underlying policy tilts toward enforcement. The memo, despite its enforcement posture, still imposes internal obligations on ICE officers. It still requires consultation with the Office of the Principal Legal Advisor (OPLA) before enforcement action is taken in cases involving potential or known victims. That means *any* enforcement action — i.e., even an arrest — is supposed to be cleared with OPLA in such cases.

It still requires deconfliction, meaning officers should affirmatively analyze whether enforcement will interfere with ongoing investigations, victim cooperation, or broader federal priorities including active trafficking prosecutions.

Those are not suggestions buried in a footnote. They are procedural safeguards embedded in ICE's own directive. When ICE fails to document that it followed those steps, the enforcement action itself becomes vulnerable. Hold their feet to the fire. That is your procedural opening. Force them to justify the omission on the record. If ICE officers bypassed their internal directives, you should expose that failure to the immigration judge. If they are legitimate and trained ICE officers, they should follow their directive, and if they are not, then a judge needs to know about it.

On May 20, 2026, in *ICWC v. Noem*, the U.S. District Court for the Central District of California issued a nationwide preliminary injunction halting ICE's "De Facto Revocation" and "Blind Removal" practices. The court prohibited ICE from disregarding grants of deferred action issued by USCIS by arresting, detaining, or removing noncitizen survivors as though their deferred action had been revoked without notice or an opportunity to be heard. The injunction also blocked ICE from carrying out removals of individuals with pending T visa, U visa, or VAWA petitions who had requested a stay of removal before USCIS had made the statutorily required prima facie eligibility determination. The court concluded that these enforcement practices undermined the humanitarian protections established by Congress. These are important protections, and we will need to continue to follow the litigation as it continues and advocate for client protections.

While this litigation continues, practitioners may cite *ICWC v. Noem* protections for T visa applicants. For example, if a client presents a T visa case receipt, the ICE officer should be prepared to go through deconfliction; they should not be blind to the person having a pending case; and they should not try to remove someone with a bonafide pending T visa case. Attorneys can counsel their clients about what defenses they have if they have an ICE encounter, and as there is litigation ongoing about which guidance should apply (as of today, it is the more protective guidance under *ICWC v. Noem),* we need to explain both the 2025 directive and the 2026 injunction.

Reframe the Argument

The first instinct in T visa removal defense might be to lead with the client's victimization and ask for mercy. Humanizing your client is always part of the work. But perhaps another litigation strategy is to shift the frame from "please protect my client" to "ICE failed to follow its own rules." T visas, deferred action, and administrative closure are statutory rights and forms of equitable legal relief designed specifically to protect victims and remedy systemic abuses. Trafficking survivors should be framed as individuals asserting their rights to legal protection, not individuals begging for mercy.

Courts respond to procedural defects. Immigration judges respond to procedural defects. Federal district court judges responding to habeas petitions respond to procedural defects. When you can show that ICE moved against your client without documented OPLA consultation, without a deconfliction analysis, and without any apparent consideration of the trafficking indicators already in the record, you are no longer just asking for discretion. You are pointing at a concrete failure of the government process.

Build that into your record early. At the intake and screening stage, document every trafficking indicator clearly. Note any cooperation your client has offered or is prepared to offer. Flag the case explicitly as one requiring deconfliction. Then, in court, ask the government to produce evidence that consultation and deconfliction actually occurred. Demand it in writing. Put it on the record that you are demanding it. You might find out that the attorney representing ICE is caught off guard. Present *ICWC v. Noem* and remind the court and opposing counsel that the "blind" and "de facto" practices by ICE are barred under a preliminary injunction and that opposing counsel (for DHS) can and should seek an expedite of your T visa applicant's bonafide determination decision.

If the government cannot answer those questions or cannot produce documentation showing that required steps were taken, the enforcement action is on weaker footing. That weakness becomes a discretionary factor, a basis for challenging detention, and in federal court, a potential claim.

Ethics Issues for Government Attorneys in Removal Court

The cleanest version of this argument, and frankly the one I find most satisfying to make as it involves professional ethics, is this: the government cannot create the problem and then use the problem as justification for removal.

If USCIS has not yet produced a BFD or has denied a BFD, that does not absolve ICE from deconfliction before taking enforcement action. If ICE hasn't completed deconfliction, they should not be making an arrest, they should not be arguing in court through OCC/OPLA that removal proceedings should continue. Rather, they should be asking for termination or a continuance so they can internally regroup and make sure they are following their own procedures, right? If they haven't completed deconfliction with state, local, federal, and internally, then they should not be putting your client on a plane.

If ICE bypassed its own deconfliction requirement, failed to coordinate with the agency adjudicating your client's T visa, and then argues that your client should be removed because no T visa has been approved yet, that argument should not stand. ICE is part of the same federal enforcement apparatus (DHS) that is supposed to be providing victim-based relief. ICE's own failure to engage that system cannot then be offered as a reason to deport the person the system was designed to protect.

The government cannot speak out of both sides of their mouth without creating an issue preclusion/*res judicata* problem. USCIS is part of DHS and DHS is part of the Immigration Court process so they should not say someone should be protected and then say they should be removed. Margalli-Olvera v. INS, 43 F.3d 345, 353 (8th Cir. 1994); United States v. McBride, 571 F. Supp. 596, 616 (D. C. Tex. 1983) ("The courts have asserted the public interest in holding the government to its word in cases of agreements not to prosecute which were entered fairly.)

Make that argument clear. Make it early. Put it in your brief, your motions, your bond hearing, and if it comes to it, your habeas petition. Cite the directive itself. Cite the TVPA's statutory purpose of encouraging victim cooperation.

Fundamental Fairness

There is active litigation right now challenging the government's rollback of victim-centered enforcement protections. Organizations have filed suits arguing that rescinding affirmative protections for trafficking victims without notice-and-comment rulemaking violates the Administrative Procedure Act. Some of that litigation is still working its way through the federal courts, and the outcomes are genuinely uncertain.

On May 20, 2026, in *ICWC v. Noem*, Judge Birotte Jr. certified three nationwide classes of U, T, and VAWA petitioners and put into place an injunction that granted temporary protections for the class members while this litigation regarding ICE policies continues. Critically, the judge ordered that the 2025 ICE guidance that had removed some protections for people pursuing T/U/VAWA cases, be rescinded. The plaintiffs who had been wrongfully deported by ICE seek to return to the U.S. While this litigation continues, you can advocate for your clients that even under the 2025 policy, your client deserves protection from removal; and you can present the current status of the litigation which includes the protective injunction that applies nationally.

You do not have to wait for a U.S. Circuit Court to hand you a clean win before you make these arguments in front of your judge.

Fundamental fairness is a principle that lives inside the immigration court system independent of any particular memo or directive. If the government bypasses its own procedural requirements, when it moves against a trafficking victim without deconfliction, without OPLA consultation, without any documented analysis of victim status, you are standing on solid ground when you say that what happened here was not fair, not lawful, and not consistent with the statutory purpose of the TVPA. Prior to the class action order, individual attorneys were already filing lawsuits to protect their individual clients or to bring them back if they were unlawfully removed.

Judges notice when the government ignores its own rules. Make sure the judge knows those rules exist, what they require, and exactly where the government has fallen short. That record matters, even if your judge rules against you today.

A Few Practical Notes on Client Communication in these High-Stakes Situations

Return calls fast. Aim to return calls the same day or at least let them know the message was received and a team member is working on a response. You don't need to have all the answers. You do not have a crystal ball. You or a team member can pick up the phone and say, "I hear you, I'm on it, here's what I know right now."

Never promise an outcome. Ever. Not "you'll be fine," not "they won't arrest you," not "this always works." What you can say is that you will work hard and keep them informed of their rights as victims and survivors.

Your representation agreement should be clear about what is and is not included. Does your fee cover emergency bond hearings? Removal defense court appearances? Appeals? Spell it out before anything goes sideways. If your agreement does not include removal defense and you are only on the T visa petition itself, make it clear. Define the scope of representation explicitly before an enforcement crisis occurs. If you do not have a removal defense part of your practice, you may even want to refer them to a removal defense attorney who can put a protective plan in place while you prepare and file their T case, so there is less to do in a rush, in case of a crisis.

During consultations, try to spend the time to go through questions about potential denial. *What happens if this is denied? What if you're detained before we get an answer?* Clients deserve to think through those scenarios before they commit to filing. If it were me sitting in that chair, I would want to know the worst-case scenario alongside the best, and I would still move forward if the potential for freedom outweighed the risk of the status quo. But others may feel differently, and their tolerance for risk or different types of risk, or the timing of taking risks, may be completely different.

Rescreening Failed Cases of Many Types for T Eligibility as Part of Your Removal Defense Plan

Once you truly understand the expansive nature of the T visa, you will realize that your law firm is likely sitting on some old, rejected, or stalled cases that actually qualify for humanitarian relief.

You should implement a system for rescreening your old files through the modern T visa framework. This is how you transform your practice and unlock relief for clients who thought they were out of options. Some may not be happy to hear from you; some phone numbers may have changed; some may not understand why you want to reach back out. You may not be successful contacting everyone, and that is no different than when we wanted to reach out to former clients and explain that new programs had opened up, like the DACA program in

2012 or the provisional I-601A waiver when that regulation was promulgated.

That there are new regulations being implemented in 2025 and 2026 is exciting, and I believe if you rescreen old cases or even just look back at your old notes with your new T-visa lenses, you will see progress. Whenever a T visa approval comes through for someone who had retained us after a re-screen, I feel very happy that they and we invested the extra time and effort in new consultations.

Rescreening Your Caseload: An Exercise

Grab a pen. Or open a notes document. Let's do another exercise. Think back through your caseload — current clients, closed files, consultations that went nowhere, cases you handed off, cases you quietly shelved because the path forward wasn't clear. I want you to start building a list of names, not to act on immediately, but to sit with. We'll work through the categories together, and by the end, I think you'll have more names on that list than you expected.

Category One: Medical Deferred Action Cases

Immigration lawyers reach for Medical Deferred Action when a client or their child faces a catastrophic health crisis. It's a reasonable instinct. The problem is that it's a temporary fix with no pathway to permanent status, and lawyers often file it without ever asking how the client got hurt or why they stayed in unsafe conditions.

If your client needs physical therapy because they fell off a roof and their employer lied about workers' compensation eligibility to force them back to work while injured — that's labor trafficking. Those medical records you're already gathering for the deferred action application? They can become powerful physical presence evidence in a T visa case.

Think also about parents of children with medical problems. A parent who is undocumented and whose child is hospitalized weekly for asthma attacks is exceptionally vulnerable to labor exploitation. They need money desperately, they're exhausted, and they cannot afford to lose a job or anger an employer. That vulnerability gets weaponized by traffickers. They may come to you only asking about medical deferred action. But you should be screening for T visa eligibility, too.

Medical deferred action doesn't lead to a green card. A T visa does.

Who on your list came to you first about a medical issue — theirs or a child's? Write down those names.

1.

2.

3.

Category Two: Military Family Cases

When a potential client presents as the undocumented partner of an active-duty service member or veteran, the instinct is to fast-track them toward Parole in Place (Military PIP or "MPIP") or another military family benefit.

However, military status can be a weapon. An abuser with rank and authority has access to an arsenal of coercive tools. Threats about reporting immigration status, threats about what happens to benefits or housing if the partner leaves, threats about what military connections can do — these are mechanisms of coercive control that can trap someone in domestic involuntary servitude or commercial sex trafficking.

You will never see any of this if you conduct the consultation with both partners in the room. I cannot stress this enough. Separate the interview. Always.

And if the relationship is a healthy and supportive one, you can still screen for both Military PIP and a T visa, right?

Maybe the potential client was victimized at a prior job, or by a partner, before falling in love with someone in the military. Maybe the potential client was excluded from Military PIP due to immigration violations or criminal history, so the T visa will be the main focus even in a supportive marriage.

With USCIS potentially issuing an NTA against a person whose PIP case is denied, and with PIP cases not having the same protections as a T visa applicant might have, it is worth considering both/any/all options.

Who on your list is a military family case you never screened alone or a military case that could not go forward due to inadmissibility issues? Write those names down.

1.

2.

3.

Category Three: Cold U Visa Certification Cases

Every humanitarian immigration attorney has a folder of U visa cases where the law enforcement certification never came. The detective didn't call back. The agency had a policy against signing. The chief said no. The case stalled or was closed while the client remained in limbo or feeling disillusioned with the system's inability to protect them.

Call those clients back. The T visa doesn't require a signed law enforcement certification. Under the "any credible evidence standard," you are empowered to build the case yourself. The power shifts from a reluctant police department back to you and your client.

T visa law and policy has also evolved significantly in recent years, which means a fresh consultation isn't just courteous, it's professionally necessary. What wasn't viable five years ago may be viable today.

Pull up that folder. Write down 3 names to start.

1.

2.

3.

Category Four: Pre-Entry Trafficking Cases

Did you once turn away a client because their trafficking happened before their last (final) entry into the United States? The current regulations have addressed this more explicitly. Physical presence is about where your client is now and why they remain here — not about who brought them across which border when.

Contact that client. The law is more favorable now.

Write down anyone to whom you previously didn't offer a T because the trafficking was not after the very last entry to the USA.

1.

2.

3.

Category Five: DACA and TPS Holders

DACA and TPS are inherently temporary. They always have been. If your client is relying on either program as their only foothold in this country, you owe them a complete humanitarian screening. These clients are often deeply embedded in communities, working, raising children, building lives — and also, sometimes, surviving exploitation they have never named out loud.

A T visa offers something DACA and TPS cannot: a pathway to permanent residence.

Who on your DACA and TPS lists have you never formally screened for trafficking indicators?

1.

2.

3.

One More Thing: The APA Challenge

If you have a client whose T visa was denied on hardship grounds or because USCIS incorrectly determined that their experience didn't constitute trafficking — and that denial came down less than six years ago — there may be grounds for a federal court challenge under the Administrative Procedure Act.

An APA challenge doesn't re-litigate the facts from scratch. It asks the federal court to review whether USCIS acted arbitrarily, capriciously, or contrary to law. If the agency applied the wrong legal standard, ignored credible evidence, or failed to adequately explain its reasoning, that denial may be reversible.

Don't let a denial be the final word. Look at the date. Look at the reasoning. Then call your client. I had a situation where we lost a case for T status over a physical presence issue. We sued 5 years later and won. No new facts. USCIS reopened the T visa case *sua sponte* and issued a T visa approval notice, such that we could withdraw our lawsuit. In other cases, we have filed a lawsuit related to a T visa denial and USCIS agreed to reopen the case but then issued an RFE for us to respond to; or the court ordered the case to be reopened by USCIS and remanded for further action such as a decision on the I-192 waiver.

If you're not comfortable with lawsuits, you may want to team up with someone more comfortable in federal court to challenge the T visa case denial that you are consulting on.

The T visa denials I have seen seem rife with errors. Usually the errors are USCIS errors, but denial letters can be harshly worded and make the lawyer and client feel horrible. Challenging a T visa denial can be an amazing solution rather than refiling, though sometimes we have done both.

If the T visa denial is based on “this is not trafficking” or “physical presence” or “hardship,” we often will pursue the APA challenge in court. If it is based on the I-192 waiver, it is often something to take to the AAO.

Congrats! You have an action plan for reaching out!

I want you to sit with the lists you made while reading this book. You've got a framework now, and an action plan.

Those names represent people who may have been surviving something you hadn't yet seen. That's not a failure of character — it's a gap in training that this book exists to close in a world where often T visa content was limited to the last 5 minutes of a 1-hour CLE.

T visa practice rewards exactly the kind of lawyering you already do: careful listening, thorough documentation, ethical advocacy under pressure. The legal framework is learnable. The screening skills sharpen with every consultation. The cases that once felt impossible start revealing themselves as ones you can actually win.

8
ETHICS AND CONFIDENTIALITY

The Shield of Confidentiality in T Visa Cases

Confidentiality is the foundation of the attorney-client relationship. When representing a survivor of human trafficking, however, it transcends legal ethics and becomes a matter of physical and emotional safety.

Your Potential Client or Client Needs to be Alone for Consultations.

During the initial screening and throughout the entire legal consultation, it is imperative that you establish strict boundaries regarding who is allowed to be in the room or on the phone. You must not let family members (especially those who are highly controlling or insist on speaking for the client) get on the phone to speak for the client. We encounter situations where a family member tries to insert themselves into the consultation, demanding to know what is being discussed or attempting to control the narrative. It can be frustrating to hear that another law firm lets the whole family into consultations or does a consultation "for everyone at the same time."

Without a confidential consultation, it is harder to know if the words spoken in the consultation belong to your client or if they were words put into the mouth of your client by others. You also never know what your client is hiding because they've been too ashamed to ever tell anyone, especially not their family or their spouse.

You never know if that friend or family member is actually the trafficker, or if their mere presence is coercing the client into silence about domestic servitude or sexual abuse. Even if that third party is well-meaning, they cannot be permitted to speak on behalf of the future client, nor should they be allowed to dominate or control the consultation process.

You should be understanding but firm, strictly enforcing the rule that the legal team needs to speak solely with the potential client in a private space. Keep in mind that some cultural expectations (such as involving elders in decisions) may need to be addressed regarding confidentiality procedures for your office.

Our booking team regularly has to tell third parties and family members that the best thing they can do is to please just let us do our job and allow the potential client the hours we need on the phone to do screening. We model our consultation confidentiality policy after the ABA brochure called "*Why Am I Left In The Waiting Room*?" You can find a copy of that here: https://www.americanbar.org/products/inv/brochure/21100 8886/ and adapt it to your practice.

With virtual (e.g., phone or video) consultations, the concept is similar whereby only the potential client or client may be on the phone. We spend extra time explaining confidentiality before beginning a call and ask if they are alone and in a safe place, with no one listening, before we begin.

We have handled consultations where the potential client is sitting parked in a car by themselves on a phone, or quietly by a sleeping baby alone at home, or hiding in a closet so that they can have a bit of privacy.

Some amount of flexibility by the consultation booking team and attorney is needed, such as situations when a baby wakes up or is distracting the person from being able to speak in a focused way, so rescheduling may be needed. I would rather reschedule a call so that childcare can be planned for a second attempt at a private call, than be in a situation where I am not sure the person was able to listen or focus. Our booking team also understands that if we break rules for consultation privacy, then people will talk in the community and say things like "another person could have their father with them for this call, why can't I?" So consistency in office policy can be more easily applied, we are more willing to offer rescheduling than we are to bend a policy about who can be on the phone. I have had clients share that the only one listening is their pet dog or cat. Pets can provide a grounding, comforting presence during difficult conversations, while human family members must remain off the call.

Another common reaction to a rescheduling offer is that the client or potential client will make sure that day they arrange for a caretaker and to be alone.

I used to think we needed to see people in person for each session, but for the number of calls we do to screen one potential new client, our phone call system has worked well. We may hear this is the first time the person has been speaking to a lawyer alone. We may hear this is the first time the potential client has ever told us about their experiences of exploitation, and that not even their spouse or mother knows about it. We could not do this without having truly confidential consultations. Careful listening is important.

Sometimes I have heard a car door or wind blowing as though a person is driving. We will need to reschedule if the person was planning on talking while driving. As a safety issue and to allow a person to focus on the important questions we have, we do not have consultations when someone is driving, even if they are on speaker phone. We also do not want a person parked on the side of the road, as a person needs to be alone and in a safe place at the time of the call.

Recitals of confidentiality matter: Reciting the protection of confidentiality in simple ways before asking difficult questions can help. For example, if I believe we are going to have to discuss a delicate criminal issue or fraud waivers, it helps to remind the client that the consultation is confidential.

> **Pro Tip**: It may be obvious to you, but starting out the call with a greeting and introducing yourself and that you are a licensed attorney is important. Whether it is the initial consultation or a later follow up call, introductions help establish each time the protections of confidentiality so that the client or potential client is reassured. "Just before we begin, I wanted to cover confidentiality again. My name is Helen Tarokic. I am an attorney licensed in North Carolina. Today's consultation is confidential, meaning we will not reveal your information without your permission, and that this call is protected by law."

Exceptions to Confidentiality in Immigration Practice

Exceptions to the general confidentiality rules come up in immigration practice, and they come up in ways that can catch you off guard if you haven't thought through them in advance.

Check your own state bar's rules. What follows reflects North Carolina's Rule 1.6, which I practice under, but the architecture of these exceptions is similar across most states. Know your jurisdiction. In North Carolina we have an ethics hotline we can call or email before taking action, and it is a great way to get some advice before overstepping or doing less than needed.

The baseline rule is simple: you don't reveal what your client tells you. Rule 1.6 (a) says, "A lawyer shall not reveal information acquired during the professional relationship with a client unless the client gives informed consent."

But Rule 1.6(b) identifies a narrow set of circumstances where disclosure is permitted, not required in most cases, but permitted. The distinction between "may" and "must" matters enormously here.

The Crime Prevention Exception

In trafficking cases, this one may surface in a specific and very human way. A client is terrified. They have lived under threat for months or years. Now they are sitting with you, or on the phone with you, and the reality of what it means to put their name on a declaration and cooperate with law enforcement is starting to land.

"I can't say that. I'll just say it didn't happen that way."

Or: "If they ask me in court, I'm going to tell them I don't remember."

Or sometimes, more quietly: "I'll just say whatever keeps me safe."

What you are hearing is a person contemplating perjury. Not because they are dishonest, but because they are scared. The trafficker is still out there. The family is still vulnerable. The threat, real or perceived, has not gone away just because they found an attorney.

Your first move is to name what you are hearing. "It sounds like you're worried about what happens if you tell the truth. Can we talk about that?" Most of the time, the statement is not an active plan to commit a crime. It is a cry for more reassurance and more information about victim rights and the legal process. The client needs to know what protections exist, what law enforcement can and cannot do with their information, and what the actual consequences of false testimony look like, including that it could destroy the very case you are building together.

Rule 1.6(b)(2) does permit disclosure to prevent a client from committing a crime, and perjury is a crime. But you are almost never at that threshold in a first conversation. You are at the threshold of a client who needs more information and more support before they can commit to telling the truth in full. Also remember that for T visa cases, the law enforcement cooperation requirement is a "reasonable person" standard, and the "person" is supposed to be a reasonable person in your client's shoes — the person who is afraid, who needs guidance, and who is facing tough decisions.

If the conversation does escalate, if a client is describing a concrete plan to fabricate testimony in a proceeding that is already scheduled, that is when I would call the ethics hotline at the North Carolina State Bar and follow their guidance.

I may let the client know that we are going to ask for help from the ethics hotline confidentially, without using their name, and discuss the matter internally with my team (sometimes with a criminal defense attorney) to see what we can do about the fear-driven planning and avoid the commission of perjury. Usually if clients trust us they are willing to help us to help them find an ethical solution, and if they won't, then we would have to follow our ethical rules of professional responsibility for our next steps. Sometimes the result with my client may be a conversation with permission about the need for the LEA's victim witness advocate to provide more support; or if there is no victim witness advocate, we need to be able to explain the limits of the ability to cooperate with testimony when there is too much fear to proceed. The bottom line is we cannot stay on a case if the person is going to commit perjury, so we want to look for solutions that allow us to proceed truthfully.

Declarations and Candor

Candor to the Tribunal (Rule 3.3 for NC) is not just a litigation rule. USCIS adjudications qualify as tribunal proceedings under the North Carolina State Bar's definition. That means the candor obligations that apply in a courtroom also apply when I am submitting a declaration to USCIS. If my client tells me the declaration is true and I know it contains material falsehoods, I cannot submit it. In that same regard, attorneys do need to ensure that their client has read the entire declaration (often meaning it has been read to them line by line by an interpreter in the client's best language) and document the dates this was done correctly.

Here is what may occur in practice. A client and I have spent hours building the declaration. They have told me things they have never told anyone. We have worked through the timeline together, verified details against medical records and text messages, and they have signed off on a draft. Then, two weeks before filing, something changes.

"I need to change that part about my boss threatening to call immigration. I don't think he said it exactly like that."

Sometimes that is legitimate. Memory is reconstructive, especially in trauma survivors. New details emerge. Old details sharpen or soften. That is normal and that is not perjury. We revise, we note why, and we move forward. It may have been a minor change like, "*My boss said we were all illegals and to watch it, which I took to mean he would call immigration if we didn't put up with his rules.*" If clarifying the sentence that way is more accurate, it is worth spending the time on it.

But sometimes what I am hearing is fear talking. The trafficker has resurfaced. A family member has applied pressure. The client is calculating what feels safer in this moment rather than what is true. The story starts shifting in ways that are internally inconsistent, that contradict the medical records, which dissolve the very elements we need to prove.

My first step is always the private conversation. Not accusatory. Not panicked. I slow everything down and name what I am observing.

"I'm noticing the timeline is changing in a few places. Help me understand what you're remembering now versus before."

Most of the time, that conversation reveals fear, not fabrication. We can work with fear. We can add safety planning, adjust the filing timeline, involve a social worker, revisit what law enforcement protections look like. I cannot file a declaration that is materially false.

If persuasion fails and the client insists on testimony I know is false, NC Rule 3.3 requires remedial measures, up to and including withdrawal. I would call the ethics hotline before I get there, and in your state you may wish to develop this practice so that you consistently get help as you build your T visa practice and encounter any manner of ethics questions for the first time.

Fear-driven threats to commit perjury usually indicate acute trauma or ongoing coercion, rather than a character flaw. They often tell you the client does not yet feel safe enough to tell the truth.

Victim declaration drafting and T visa case preparation involves reviewing and checking every word and question with the client and addressing issues that are trauma-related in the process.

Reasonably Certain Death or Bodily Harm

Rule 1.6(b)(3) permits disclosure to prevent reasonably certain death or substantial bodily harm. This is the exception to confidentiality that worries me the most.

Picture this: a client calls you after hours, clearly terrified, and discloses that her trafficker has threatened to kill her and her children if she does not return to the house where she was held. She is not asking you to call the police. She may actively not want you to. But you are now sitting with information suggesting imminent, serious danger.

This is where trauma-informed practice and professional ethics intersect. You are permitted to disclose confidential information (but please check your state bar rules first and, again, the ethics hotline is often critical here). Whether you disclose that confidential information, and how, involves factors including whether the threat is credible and specific, whether there are other protective options, and what your client's own safety plan looks like. Your first move is still to talk with your client.

If Legal Services Were Used to Commit Fraud

In North Carolina, Ethics Rule 1.6(b)(4) covers the scenario where a lawyer's services were used as an instrument of a client's crime or fraud. In immigration practice, this might look like discovering, mid-representation, that a client gave you false information that you unwittingly submitted to USCIS. You have a right, not a duty, to take steps to rectify that situation, which may require disclosure.

This is distinct from the situation where a trafficking survivor has prior fraud in their history that you are handling through an I-192 waiver. That is disclosed intentionally and ethically with the client's full knowledge and consent. The Rule 1.6(b)(4) scenario is for fraud you didn't know about when you acted on it.

I've had situations where we have had to withdraw and/or make a disclosure to the tribunal. I was fortunate to have our NC ethics hotline at hand, and also there are good attorneys in my state to refer a client to for crimmigration/criminal defense. In some situations, we were able to simply amend the application that was pending and explain what happened, and I have been grateful to see positive immigration outcomes in those situations. Conflicts, confidentiality, client identification, and capacity/duress issues will need analysis each time, and that all brings us back to remembering to have good office policies in place that put honesty and compassion first.

I will not deny that this is all time consuming. However, as you do more and more humanitarian work that helps you understand better human nature and typical ethical scenarios that come up, you should find these situations less startling and more like ones you have seen before. You will know how to handle them and when to ask for help.

The Practical Takeaway for Immigration Consultations.

Most of the time, none of the confidentiality exceptions activate in practice at our law firm. Most of what your clients tell you stays protected, and your job is to protect it vigorously. Understanding these exceptions matters for two reasons.

First, knowing they exist helps you recognize the rare situation when you are actually facing one, rather than freezing or, worse, acting without thinking it through.

Second, and this is particularly true in trafficking cases, understanding these limits helps you explain confidentiality accurately to clients. You can tell a client that what they share is protected, while being honest that there are narrow situations involving imminent serious harm where the rules permit limited disclosure. Most clients, including trafficking survivors who have lived under systems of total information control, find that kind of accurate, clear explanation more reassuring than an unqualified promise. They have been lied to by others. However, a realistic explanation of what you will and won't do, and why, builds more trust than a sweeping guarantee.

When in doubt, call your state bar's ethics hotline. That's what it is there for.

Unnecessary Secrets — Access to Case Status and File Copies

Sending your client a copy of what you filed, when you filed it, is not optional generosity. It is baseline professional practice. In T visa cases specifically, this matters beyond ethics.

Your client's trafficker may have confiscated their documents, monitored calls, and weaponized access to information about their own life against them in the past. Keeping your client in the dark about their own immigration case — even unintentionally, even just because your office hasn't built a system for it — replicates a dynamic of control that trafficking produced.

In my past experiences as a business immigration attorney, I was always surprised that, for example, law offices would not give copies of the H-1B filing to the foreign national, claiming the file belonged to the sponsoring business petitioner. Yet, if it were time for visa stamping, the copy would be provided right before the foreign national had to fly to their home country for a consular interview — a very late stage to be giving a person a copy of critical documents. Why not provide it all early on, so that everyone is on equal footing?

In the T visa context, I am hard pressed to think of a situation where copies of the filing should not be provided to the client, unless there is some extraordinary circumstance. For example, mailing hard copies to a home where the person is abused may be unsafe, but sending them electronically can still happen, and we ask our clients to change passwords and usernames securely if they have any concerns.

In T visa representation you should confidentially send copies of everything you file to the client, every receipt notice USCIS generates, every piece of correspondence that comes in. Explain what each document means in plain language, in the client's best language, with interpreter support when needed. If and when the bona fide determination arrives, explain again what it means, as a lot of time may have passed since the case was originally filed. If a Request for Evidence arrives, call and email, and explain what the opportunity to respond to the RFE will mean and any associated costs. Clients should know where their case stands because we build that transparency into the representation from day one. It takes time, but it is worth it.

Clients who understand their own case are better witnesses, better partners in building their declaration, and better prepared for what comes next. They are less likely to panic and make fear-driven decisions when something unexpected happens, because they trust that you will tell them what is happening in real time.

Check your state's rules on file access and delivery. Build the systems now, before a client has to ask.

A client who has to beg for a copy of their own filing has experienced something they have likely experienced before. A client who has to beg you for a copy of their own filing may experience retraumatization. Don't be another person who denied them control over their own life.

Therapist Confidentiality: A Different Shield, Same Principle

Clients may not know what therapy is, and the connection between you explaining your representation is confidential and also asking them if they are willing to participate in therapy. On the one hand we are saying the case is mostly between us and USCIS, with some limited reasonable cooperation with law enforcement if law enforcement were to respond to our report. On the other we are saying "here is a referral to a therapist or clinic where the client may talk to a mental health provider about their trafficking victimization. For a confidential and deeply private matter, it seems like a lot of people are involved.

It is also possible the client never had access to mental health care, or they come from countries where therapy carries stigma, or the word has been weaponized against them.

I've had clients who thought that if I asked their therapist for a letter confirming attendance dates, I was somehow pulling recordings of their sessions or reading the therapist's private clinical notes. That is not what we do, and it is not what we are asking for.

A therapist has their own confidentiality obligations, governed by their professional licensing board and, in most cases, HIPAA. What we typically request from a treating therapist is a limited release of information — specifically, confirmation that the client is actively engaged in treatment, the general nature of services being provided, and the dates of attendance. That's it. We are not asking the therapist to turn over session notes. We are not asking what the client said about their trafficker or their childhood or their marriage. We ask for what helps us document physical presence and ongoing recovery for the T visa record, and nothing more.

The therapist should walk them through what a limited release authorization actually authorizes before they sign it.

Therapists, for their part, also operate under exceptions to confidentiality, and many of them are structurally similar to ours. A therapist's intake paperwork will include forms explaining when those exceptions apply — mandatory reporting for child abuse, duty to warn when a client poses a credible threat of harm to an identified person, situations involving imminent self-harm. Therapists tend to be further along than attorneys in normalizing this conversation with clients, perhaps because their practice more routinely involves acute mental health crises where those exceptions are triggered. They have thought through how to explain these limits to a frightened person in plain language, and many of them are quite good at it.

When I refer a client to a therapist who works with trafficking survivors, I make sure the client understands that the therapist's confidentiality rules protect them too — and that our offices are not pooling information beyond what the client has specifically authorized us to share.

Other Ethical Issues to Watch For

Here are a few situations I have encountered, heard about from colleagues, or seen surface in discussions at trainings. Some of them are uncomfortable to name out loud, but that's exactly why we need to name them.

USCIS is Supposed to Process T Visa Confidentiality

Once you take the case, that shield of confidentiality extends into the federal immigration system. The law provides robust privacy protections under 8 U.S.C. 1367, which specifically restricts the use and disclosure of information relating to applicants for T nonimmigrant status. USCIS processes T visa applications confidentially, and we have all correspondence go to our office, as the safe address listed on the G-28 attorney representation form.

This statutory shield strictly prohibits the government from sharing your client's sensitive information with third parties, ensuring that abusers and traffickers cannot manipulate the federal government to locate or further harm the victim. When you explain this level of confidentiality to a potential client, it often gives them the sense of safety they need to finally step forward and tell their complete story. It is your ethical duty to explain how this protection works so that your client can make a truly informed decision about pursuing a T visa.

It is easy to forget to explain the confidentiality rules about T visa filings with USCIS, if it is not a standard part of your consultation when discussing T visa work. If you run out of the time in the call, it can be addressed in a follow up session.

Here is the section from the T visa regulation on confidentiality:

> "8 CFR § 214.216 Restrictions on use and disclosure of information relating to applicants for T nonimmigrant classification.
> (a) The use or disclosure (other than to a sworn officer or employee of DHS, the Department of Justice, the Department of State, or a bureau or agency of any of those departments, for legitimate department, bureau, or agency purposes) of any information relating to the beneficiary of a pending or approved Application for T Nonimmigrant Status is prohibited unless the disclosure is made in accordance with an exception described in 8 U.S.C. 1367(b).
> (b) Information protected under 8 U.S.C. 1367(a)(2) may be disclosed to Federal prosecutors to comply with constitutional obligations to provide statements by witnesses and certain other documents to defendants in pending Federal criminal proceedings.
> c) Agencies receiving information under this section, whether governmental or non-governmental, are bound by the confidentiality provisions and other restrictions set out in 8 U.S.C. 1367.
> (d) DHS officials are prohibited from making adverse determinations of admissibility or deportability based on information obtained solely from the trafficker, unless the applicant has been convicted of a crime or crimes listed in section 237(a)(2) of the Act."

That said, what happens if the government violates confidentiality provisions? There are civil fines as well as disciplinary action (like job termination) for federal employees or contractors who violate the protections of U.S.C. 1367.

Can I Represent Both the Employer and the Worker?

If a worker has a potential T visa claim arising from their employment relationship, you likely cannot represent the employer in the same matter, and you likely cannot represent them in related matters either. The conflict is not theoretical. The employer may be the trafficker, or at minimum, a witness or adverse party. Run your conflict check early, before you take either representation. As always, you can run conflict questions through your state bar ethics hotline program.

What if the Client has not Escaped Their Trafficker?

This happens more than practitioners expect, and it can feel destabilizing when it does. Your job is not to rescue the client, and as the attorney you are not to take the role of law enforcement nor therapist. Your job is to give them accurate legal information and let them make informed decisions about their own lives, subject to the confidentiality rules and exceptions governing the practice of law.

You can document your advice, explain the risks, and continue to make yourself available.

T visa applicants are able to establish physical presence on account of trafficking including in situations where they are currently being subjected to a severe form of trafficking in persons. The USCIS T visa regulations and T Visa Policy Manual already address this issue, meaning they do not expect everyone to have ended the trafficking victimization before applying for T visa status.

What if the Trafficker Threatens to Report My Client?

When a trafficker or their attorney threatens to report your client to immigration authorities unless they abandon a civil claim, stay silent, or settle for nothing, it may be a serious ethical violation and also may have criminal consequences for the person making the threat.

North Carolina specifically addressed this in **2005 Formal Ethics Opinion 3**, which examined whether a defense lawyer could pressure a plaintiff into settlement negotiations by threatening to report undocumented status discovered during civil discovery.

The answer was no.

Understanding the State Bar's analysis is crucial, as it applies to T visa practice. The opinion clarifies that threats of criminal prosecution related to a civil matter, even without an explicit rule prohibiting them, remain unethical due to obligations against conduct prejudicial to justice and using means solely to embarrass, intimidate, harass, or coerce.

Your client's immigration status doesn't affect the valuation of a wage theft or personal injury claim, making its introduction in negotiations unjust. Threatening to report undocumented status during civil negotiations is prohibited as a result.

As we previously discussed, "abuse of the legal process" constitutes coercion for involuntary servitude. Threatening deportation within civil proceedings is thus both coercive and unethical.

What if My Client Wants a Promise or Guarantee?

Our new Constitution is now established, and has an appearance that promises permanency; but in this world nothing can be said to be certain, except death and taxes.

— Benjamin Franklin, in a letter to Jean-Baptiste Le Roy, 1789

You should not promise your client that USCIS will approve their case. That sounds obvious, but when you're sitting with someone who has survived something terrible and they're asking you whether this is going to work — the pressure to reassure them is real. Resist it. Even if you have won 100 cases, resist the urge to make promises.

What you can say is this: you and your team will prepare the strongest case the evidence supports. You will be clear with them about the weaknesses that you see. You will not submit anything you don't believe is true. You can discuss past results but make it clear that they may not indicate future results. This is not to wiggle out of responsibility but rather to manage expectations and demonstrate truthfulness about what you are unable to control.

Here's where it gets layered in T visa practice specifically.

On confidentiality, you can tell your client that USCIS is prohibited by statute from sharing their application information with their trafficker, their abuser, or DHS enforcement in most circumstances. What you cannot promise is that the world outside USCIS will never learn about their case. If they tell their cousin, if they post about it, if their trafficker has informants in their community — that's outside your control. Manage that expectation clearly and early.

On reporting, you cannot guarantee nor promise how law enforcement will respond. You can explain what a reasonable reporting effort looks like, help them document contact with the right agencies, and make sure they understand what cooperation means under the statute. But whether the FBI agent picks up the phone, whether the detective takes them seriously, whether anyone is ever prosecuted — none of that is in your hands or theirs. For example, I have explained in the past that one law enforcement agency never responded to our reports until one day, a year later, during a time that the agency was on furlough of all times, an agent called us back. It seemed they had been cleaning their office and found an old letter we had sent. I have explained my past experiences with particular prosecutors and police officers or department heads, but we know that people come and go, the leaders in agencies can change, and so reporting results are not something we can promise or guarantee.

On legal representation itself, be clear about the scope of your engagement. Are you handling the T visa only? What happens if a removal order surfaces — would that be a separate contract? What if derivative family members need help — is it clear your retainer does or does not include derivatives? Put it in your fee agreement. Clients in crisis tend to hear what they need to hear, and your engagement letter protects both of you.

On timelines, the current average processing time according to USCIS for July of 2026 just increased to 32+ months from filing to a final decision. It will change for better or worse over time and USCIS data may not be timely or fully accurate. Explain that government processing times shift, that your office will monitor the case, and that getting a work permit through the bona fide process is a real and meaningful milestone — but it is not approval.

Managing expectations is not pessimism.

Getting Over Your FOFT (Fear of First T)

This section on ethics and law office practices may have been stressful because it may mean changing your day-to-day law office operating procedures. I often explain I didn't have to ask so many questions before the law changed, but a change in law obligates immigration attorneys to open their minds to changing how their law practice works to ensure they are not missing out on critical options.

When you are first learning about the complexities of human trafficking, it is completely natural to experience what I call FOFT, which is the Fear of First T.

You might worry that you will make a mistake, that you will traumatize the client, or that the government will reject your legal arguments. Do not let the fear of making a mistake prevent you from taking your first T visa case. Instead, channel that anxiety into rigorous screening, keeping a vigilant eye out for the indicators of trafficking in every client interaction, and being a constant student of law.

You do not have to navigate this challenging area of law entirely on your own. You can pair up with a mentor, attend dedicated T visa trainings, and build a network of colleagues who can offer confidential case reviews in compliance with state bar rules of professional responsibility. Use your legal training, your commitment to client-centered advocacy, and your professional judgment to build the best possible case for your clients.

If another practitioner tells you not to file a T visa or warns you not to sue or appeal a bad decision, you should not be afraid to seek out multiple professional opinions, challenge the status quo, and forge your own pathway into this profoundly life-changing work. If I had listened to the first lawyer who told me not to sue, I would not have thereafter filed and won my first T visa lawsuit. I only learned later that the person who told me the lawsuit would not work had no litigation experience. When I partnered with someone who had years of litigation experience with DOJ lawsuits, and later received a supporting amicus from a non-profit, the lawsuit process for my T visa client went smoothly.

So where do we go from here?

Where do you see yourself as an attorney in 1 year? In 3 years? Take that vision and build it out. Remember, you may be new to this, but you're still a pioneer in the immigration law industry just for getting this far. You have a chance to do some of the most exciting, innovative legal work, whether it's taking one T visa case or building a section of your law practice to broaden your reach nationally into this area.

Come join our CLE programs for lawyers online (you can find us on Eventbrite.com) and we'll be so glad you did. We also invite guest speakers on issues like secondary trauma, attorney well-being, and more. If you're interested in becoming a speaker on T visa work or a related topic, please also reach out to us. There is always more room at the table.

With your can-do attitude...consider bringing in private social workers to your law practice. More on this in the next chapter.

9

Social Work Placements in Law Firms

Can-do attitudes can result in amazing partnerships: law firms can have social work field placement programs.

Consider an MSW Field Placement Program

Your immigration law firm may at some point want to consider putting in place a structured social work field placement program to help improve your humanitarian immigration law practice.

Private law firms like mine occupy this weird middle ground where we are doing the work, absorbing the cost, and yet are still disqualified from most of the funding designed to support exactly this kind of work. As a private law firm, we don't receive federal funding the way nonprofits can, and we also need to take cases that some nonprofits are restricted from taking due to their funding guidelines. Every organization is trying their best, and we all play some role, but it is frustrating when you know what might help your client, and you cannot access it for them.

There have been stretches in this work where the bureaucratic walls were exasperating. For example, finding pathways to connect clients to TVAP (the Trafficking Victims Assistance Program) was harder than it should have been due to capacity issues. Because the help a TVAP social worker can provide is so profound, it was very frustrating when there weren't placements available. Nonprofit capacity in our region was stretched to the breaking point. Pro bono slots at established organizations filled quickly.

Several years ago, I identified a local foundation with grant offerings that, as written, seemed to include us. We inquired. Shortly after, the guidelines were quietly updated to require nonprofit status. Another door closed.

One suggestion that came out of that season of frustration changed everything: team up and get an MOU with our local university to host Master of Social Work (MSW) field placement students at our firm. I was curious to see if this could really work out when a social worker at a hospital suggested it to me. It ended up being a great idea.

We were the first law firm with whom our local university structured a field placement agreement, but their MSW program already had the infrastructure for us to customize the program for our law firm — learning contracts, supervision protocols, confidentiality agreements, student insurance, stipends and reimbursements, clear expectations about macro versus micro versus hybrid practice approaches, and the MOU (Memorandum of Understanding) agreement that our firm and the university contact would need to sign.

Here is what I did not expect: the depth of what master-level social workers bring into a law office.

Their knowledge of local community resources is encyclopedic in a way no attorney I know can match, and more importantly, they know how to communicate that information in ways people receive very well. Sometimes it genuinely takes a social worker to make a warm handoff to another social worker at TVAP. That's not a flaw in the system. That's relationship-based practice working exactly as it should.

How Social Workers and Immigration Law Firms Can Help One Another

We currently have three social workers woven into how we operate — one full-time program graduate, and two current field placement interns working toward their MSW who are supervised by my full-time employee (and layered above that, attorney supervision). Watching this grow has shifted something in how I think about what a private immigration law firm can be.

Some of our placement students stay one semester. Some stay two or three, depending on their program (3 is ideal for us). That duration matters. A two-month summer internship barely gets past orientation and is not something we accept. A multi-semester placement means the student actually learns the cases, learns the clients, learns the intersections between immigration law and trauma and public benefits and health care access. They contribute. They catch things. They can participate in the next year's recruitment fair, share what they learned, and pick a great match for our future semester's placement. Since social workers build systems, they even help build your program. Social workers get along great with paralegals, and the paralegals love that when a "social work" problem comes up in our immigration law practice, they know someone who can help.

Social workers are already trained in intake/needs assessment in ways that translate beautifully to our work. When I say intake, I do not mean having them do consultation. I mean, social workers are already coming in trained in methods of assessing life history, trauma-informed interviewing, and needs assessments for the purposes of connecting people to resources that can help.

They understand medico-legal intersections — workplace injuries, mental health diagnoses, hospital discharge planning — in ways that make our case preparation stronger. The field placement interns are already highly educated, and many have an undergraduate degree in social work plus work experience by the time they are placed with us. They even have advisors to help them while they intern.

You aren't a social worker. You do not charge for social work services. You are a lawyer. Your social worker field placement match has a university supervisor. The student's university field liaison typically conducts weekly check-ins to monitor their progress and provide necessary support, which is vital given the steep learning curve and secondary trauma risks inherent in trafficking work.

The social worker interns team up together to solve problems that will make your legal work and law firm run more smoothly.

Possible Career Paths after Completing a Social Work Field Placement at an Immigration Law Firm

Consider where these MSW students can go when they leave us and graduate:

- Some become therapists. A former MSW intern later becomes a licensed clinical social worker specializing in trauma and is now the ideal future therapist for a survivor of domestic violence and human trafficking.

They already know what a T visa is. They won't accidentally tell a client something that undermines her case, and they know not to give legal advice.

- Some social workers go on to work directly for TVAP programs, bringing with them an understanding of what evidence actually helps an immigration case.

- Some end up in hospitals, schools, immigration detention facilities, courthouses, refugee resettlement agencies, or the Veterans Administration — every single one of those places where trafficking indicators go unrecognized every day.

- Some will work for DSS/child welfare offices and will now be able to identify minors who are surviving trafficking, before they age out of the system.

- One of our associates went to law school after starting as a social worker — and we now have a social worker field placement intern thinking about law school. The pipeline can run in both directions.

- MSW students will be more prepared to be competitive in getting hired after graduation. For example, MSW interns helped us with vetting therapists. That is a long process. Googling therapist names is not enough when trying to pair a client with someone who will professionally help them. When they spend time vetting therapists and getting to know everyone and anyone who can help with therapy for trafficking victims, they build relationships with their future peers prior to graduation and also get to see what the job market is lacking in terms of offerings.

The Social Worker Pipeline Effect

Every trained social worker carries trafficking awareness into systems where immigration attorneys rarely reach.

MSW Field Placement in Immigration Firm • T visa screening • Trauma-informed interviewing • TVAP coordination • Socio-medico-legal collaboration	**→ Trafficking-Informed Professional** • Recognizes force, fraud, coercion • Spots non-obvious trafficking • Understands referral pathways • Connects survivors to legal services
Therapist / Licensed Clinical Social Worker *"This is not just trauma. This may be trafficking."* → Documents trauma treatment → Refers to T visa lawyer	**Child Welfare / DSS** *"This is not just abuse. This was trafficking."* → Identifies minors who were trafficked → Connects to legal services before age out
Hospital Social Work *"This is not just an injury from a job."* → Flags exploitation → Refers to legal help	**Schools / Youth Systems** *"This is not just a behavior issue."* → Recognizes recruitment of minors → Connects minors to legal help
TVAP / Nonprofit *"This survivor needs legal help."* → Strong referrals → Aligns services	**Detention Systems** *"This may be a trafficking victim."* → Identifies victims in custody → Prevents wrongful removal
Policy / Government *"We should be screening for trafficking."* → Improves systems → Expands access	**MSW → Attorney** *"I know what trafficking looks like."* → Integrates disciplines → Adds social workers to law practice

Law Enforcement and Social Work. The Social Worker Pipeline also should include law enforcement. For example, one U/T certifier at a local law enforcement agency let me know they have social workers in their crisis division who assist victims of domestic violence, sexual assault, and other crimes. Police and Sheriff's offices, as well as Prosecutor's offices, can benefit greatly from incorporating social workers and field placements into their programs.

Outcome: Earlier Identification → Stronger Evidence → Better T Visa Cases → More Survivors Protected

This is not just about improving our firm, though it has. This is about building a broader community of professionals who understand trafficking — not as an abstraction, but as something they have seen up close, helped document, and helped survivors navigate. That ripple effect is so cool. When you do a lot of T visa work, you become acutely aware of the harsh realities of systemic exploitation, and so building a better world with more social workers attuned to immigration issues gives you a tangible way to address systemic failures.

Thinking Creatively and Partnering with Community Organizations — Some Guidelines and Structure Needed

I never imagined that a foundation turning us away over lack of nonprofit status would lead to social work field placement programs with not one but three (3) different universities that have genuinely changed how we practice and whom we can serve. Now, each of the universities we have an MOU with has a place to refer students with an interest in using social work to help immigrants.

Sidebar: they have MSW field placements at veterinary offices nowadays. For the veterinarians. Consider that MSW field placements are now utilized in veterinary offices to help veterinarians manage systemic compassion fatigue and emotional distress. If that isn't an argument for thinking creatively about who belongs in your professional space, I don't know what is. Who thought of that? Social workers!

If you haven't explored adding a social work field placement to your immigration practice, I'm telling you: look into it. The conversation alone might open a door you didn't know was there.

But if you bring a social work student in expecting a cheap paralegal, you will fail the student, you will fail your clients, you will miss the point of T visa work, and you will probably lose the partnership with the university. These students are in a rigorous graduate program. They are learning. They are being evaluated. They are also, simultaneously, genuinely contributing at a level that will astonish you once the relationship is properly structured. You need to design your field placement program to meet university requirements and stick to them.

The MOU is where it all starts. Think of it as your retainer agreement with the university. It spells out what you are committing to as a field agency and what the university is bringing to the table in return. Your obligations are real: you need a qualified field instructor, meaning someone with a social work license or, since it is a law firm, an attorney who can supervise. This is where hiring your first full-time social worker becomes a strategic move rather than just a feel-good one. Eventually we hired a full-time social worker to be the supervisor, and that has been great.

The university brings more to this than just students. They bring insurance coverage for the student's field activities, which matters. They bring an academic field advisor who checks in regularly and catches problems before they become crises. They bring a structured educational framework, the Council on Social Work Education competencies, that actually gives shape to what can otherwise feel like an overwhelming and amorphous job.

The Council on Social Work Education (CSWE) outlines nine interrelated core competencies that all social work students must achieve and demonstrate through their Learning Contract. Each of these competencies integrates dimensions of learning — specifically knowledge, values, skills, and cognitive/affective processes — and is measured through observable practice behaviors in the field.

Core Competencies Intersecting with Immigration Law Firm Needs

Here is a breakdown of the Nine Core Competencies outlined by the CSWE. As you read them, ask yourself what each one has in common with your own goals in law practice.

1. Demonstrate Ethical and Professional Behavior Social workers should understand their profession's value base, ethical standards, and relevant laws. This means using self-reflection to manage personal values, applying critical thinking to ethical decision-making, and maintaining a professional demeanor across all communications.

2. Engage Diversity and Difference in Practice *(Also framed as Anti-racism, Diversity, Equity, and Inclusion in Macro Practice)* Students should understand how intersectionality — age, class, culture, immigration status, race, and more — shapes human experience. They practice cultural humility, apply self-awareness, and recognize how oppression and discrimination operate.

3. Advance Human Rights and Social, Economic, and Environmental Justice Every person has fundamental rights: freedom, safety, privacy. Students learn theories of social justice and develop strategies to dismantle oppressive structural barriers and distribute resources equitably.

4. Engage in Practice-informed Research and Research-informed Practice Social workers use quantitative and qualitative research to evaluate effectiveness and translate findings into better interventions and policy improvements.

5. Engage in Policy Practice Policy shapes access to services at every level. Students learn to analyze, formulate, and advocate for policies that advance social and economic justice.

6. Engage with Individuals, Families, Groups, Organizations, and Communities Engagement is ongoing and interactive. Students apply theories of human behavior, use empathy and interpersonal skills, and build strong professional relationships across systems.

7. Assess Individuals, Families, Groups, Organizations, and Communities Assessment means gathering and interpreting data about a client's or community's needs, identifying strengths and challenges, and developing mutually agreed-upon intervention goals.

8. Intervene with Individuals, Families, Groups, Organizations, and Communities Students select and implement evidence-informed interventions, advocate on behalf of clients, collaborate across professions, and manage effective transitions when goals are met.

9. Evaluate Practice with Individuals, Families, Groups, Organizations, and Communities Students apply qualitative and quantitative methods to monitor outcomes, analyze effectiveness, and use what they learn to continuously improve their practice.

What Might This Mean in Practice?

When a student's learning contract identifies "advance human rights and social, economic, and environmental justice" as a competency, and you sit down together to figure out what that means concretely in your law firm, what you are actually doing is building a curriculum. You are deciding together that this student will attend a county commission meeting and present data on TVAP resource gaps and recognize a local organization (such as in our case, Lutheran Services Carolinas) for the gaps they do fill.

You are deciding that this student will map the transportation barriers that prevent your clients from accessing therapy.

You are deciding that this student will sit with a client who just received her bona fide determination letter and help her with accessing resources to learn how to drive or pass a driver's license test.

That learning contract is a framework that keeps both of you accountable and keeps the student's time from being swallowed up by whatever is loudest in your office on any given week.

Now, about the micro and macro distinction, because this will genuinely shape how you recruit and what you ask of students: If you don't really understand macro versus micro, the university professor helping you draft the learning contract, and the student you are writing it with should help you.

An advanced MSW student with a macro learning contract, mapped and presented on regional TVAP resource deserts, which changed how our team talks to clients about what they can realistically access and where. That service desert map was shared with the state human trafficking commission, and other important organizations. Students who attended our local county Hispanic and Latino Commission meetings submitted research that successfully highlighted systemic issues requiring the Commission's attention.

I'm going to give a few examples about things that would come up on the Hispanic/Latino Commission I was appointed to as a local immigration lawyer, which were not immigration issues, but which mattered for the work we do.

There was a concern that Hispanic/Latino community members needed broader access to dental care, urgently. A lack of dental care can lead to severe health problems. The solution presented was that county residents could use the local senior center for free dental help. But then, the next issues were:

- Lack of clarity about whether all Hispanic/Latino community members needing the services fit the definition of "county resident." Did "resident" for the county mean "resides here" regardless of status, or did it mean green card holding resident?

- Was there anyone there who spoke Spanish? It turned out there was no Spanish-speaking assistance to screen or to assist people needing dental services.

- It seemed the location of the dental clinic changed, and it was not widely communicated to the public. There were community resource issues.

Another issue addressed by the Hispanic/Latino Commission was that the school district phone line for Spanish was potentially being routed to a voicemail box that wasn't attended.

Another good example addressed by social workers was a resource list that included providing bikes to people for free. They periodically verified whether those services were available to people like our clients. If no one is checking that list, you don't find out if a service has ended, and you could disappoint clients referred to them for help.

No one wants to hand a resource list to a T visa client only to find out the list was useless because there was no working phone, or a place changed locations or shut down, or the place wasn't vetted for immigration status disqualifiers.

These issues were all social work issues related to commission work and related to our law firm and community. When we hand a resource list to a T visa client for help, we want to know that the information in it is good, and it's been great having social worker field interns who help find good information that might be provided to our clients. The work they did extended further into the community, too.

The therapist vetting piece also grew organically out of this because as lawyers, we absolutely wanted to connect our T visa clients with therapy, but doing that was challenging. We were already struggling to find trauma-informed therapists who understood immigration contexts well enough not to inadvertently undermine a pending T visa case. Social work students, with their clinical training and their community connections, became our best researchers for building that referral list. They knew how to evaluate a therapist's actual framework, not just their website biography. I am sure some of them will become great therapists when they graduate.

The Foundation: The MOU and What to Expect

Before a student can start changing lives in your office, you will have to navigate a little bit of university paperwork, starting with a Memorandum of Understanding (MOU), sometimes called a Memorandum of Affiliation. The MOU is the formal, legal contract between your law firm and the university that establishes the educational partnership. As a participating law firm, your general requirements include providing a qualified field instructor, offering appropriate physical workspace, and ensuring the student gets firsthand experiences that align with academic standards. On-site placements are great, and direct work in person is great, but sometimes we were asked and able to work in a hybrid setting (e.g., some days the MSW works from home, others at the office in person).

In exchange, you can expect the university to provide academic oversight, conduct periodic reviews through their Office of Academic Affairs, and typically supply structural protections like professional liability insurance for their students so your firm is not bearing that risk alone. The MOU also explicitly outlines privacy expectations, noting that while your law firm may or may not be a covered entity under HIPAA, the university students are considered "workforce" and must be strictly trained on your firm's privacy policies before accessing any Protected Health Information. These agreements generally run for a set number of years and automatically renew, allowing you to build a long-term pipeline of talent.

The Framework: CSWE Competencies and the Learning Contract

Once the MOU is signed and the semester begins, you and the student will collaboratively develop a "Learning Contract." As I mentioned, the Council on Social Work Education (CSWE) requires students to achieve nine interrelated core competencies, which include demonstrating ethical behavior, engaging diversity, advancing human rights, engaging in policy practice, and evaluating practice with individuals and communities. The Learning Contract translates these broad academic competencies into concrete, observable learning activities tailored to your law firm.

Because the learning contract is a "living document," you will use it continuously throughout the semester to guide your weekly supervision and evaluate the student's progress. Evaluation methods typically include direct observation, supervision discussions, and scaling. At the end of the semester, you will complete a formal evaluation where you rate the student's performance on a standardized scale from 0 (Incomplete) up to 5 (Advanced Competence), or the university will have given you some other rating system. This structured process ensures you are truly mentoring these students and watching them develop into fierce advocates.

I really enjoyed sitting down with our students. They have fresh energy and the struggles I had as an immigration lawyer feeling like the T visa was not enough were ameliorated by social workers who could help out in their social worker lane while I stayed in my lawyer lane.

Micro Social Work: Direct Client Interventions

When you host an MSW student with a Micro focus, their learning contract will likely lean heavily into "micro" social work, which focuses on direct, one-on-one client interventions and stabilization. A micro-focused student might be tasked with conducting needs assessments for the Trafficking Victim Assistance Program (TVAP) to understand exactly what a survivor requires or identifying alternative community resources when TVAP falls short.

Their learning activities will require them to actively use a strengths-based perspective, person-centered approach, and motivational interviewing skills to engage with clients who have experienced trauma. They will also learn practical firm mechanics, like gathering proof of therapy attendance or reviewing therapist support letters for helpful information to point out to the attorneys.

Furthermore, micro learning contracts emphasize cultural humility; you might have a student specifically work on utilizing basic Spanish skills through daily practice to better connect with your Spanish-speaking clients, fostering deep respect for diverse life experiences.

Micro program work might also include shadowing submission of, submitting, and following up on TVAP referrals, as well as connecting people with alternative resources.

Micro program work might include connecting former T visa clients, who now have green cards and are on their way to naturalization, with qualified doctors who can help evaluate them to see if their trauma/mental health may necessitate an N-648 medical exemption from citizenship tests. I've been lucky enough to see my way through the T visa and green card process to the point where some of my clients need language or testing exemptions for U.S. citizenship, and we can actually help them thanks to our expanding resource lists.

Macro Social Work: Systemic Change and Policy

Conversely, when you bring an advanced MSW student into your firm, you can utilize a "macro" learning contract that zooms out to focus on systemic change, community organization, and policy advocacy. Instead of solely doing direct client therapy, a macro student analyzes the structural injustices and resource distribution that impact your clients. As I explained earlier, a macro student might map out "resource deserts" and present to your legal team on the massive disparities in TVAP services, ensuring your staff knows exactly where clients can and cannot get help.

They might attend a human trafficking commission meeting and ask questions and present findings.

They might reach out to the Office of Trafficking in Persons and help put together recommendations for further OTIP program participation.

A macro learning contract also empowers students to leverage political capital and challenge structures of power. Your student might spearhead a civic engagement project — such as voter education — which can measurably increase voter turnout. Your student might later present statistics that 300 hours of voter education work resulted in only 8 to 10% improved voter turnout. Knowing the data and barriers to newly naturalized citizens voting is important to addressing them in future voter education programs.

Even navigating the naturalization process can be a macro activity; the student can use principles of human dignity to help non-native English speakers pass the citizenship test or identify them as potential candidates for testing exemptions, transforming a bureaucratic hurdle into an empowering life event. Our T visa clients might one day have green cards and then want to apply for citizenship, and the social and language barriers to naturalization can be reduced by having social workers involved.

If implementing a field placement program seems overwhelming for your current practice model, remember that it is entirely optional. No one has to build a program like this in their law firm. I only mention my experience in this because for a long time, I focused mostly on T visa work and kept finding gaps I wanted to fill.

If you work at a private law firm filling T visa legal services gaps, you may find that there are gaps in other areas (like TVAP connections) to work on, and you may find some joy addressing those issues when the time is right.

Other attorneys have worked on impact projects, created foundations, made donations, or have simply kept up with their immigration legal work. My interests overall have aligned with the belief that what is good for the client is good for their case. When a client is supported and feels safe, they are more capable of participating in the legal process, which ultimately strengthens our chance of success. A client-centered approach values the survivor's well-being as a primary goal in and of itself, which in turn empowers them to be active participants in their legal journey.

The "Can-Do" Lawyer's Exercise

You've just read about confidentiality walls, MSW partnerships, TVAP gaps, civic engagement projects, and everything in between. That's a lot. Somewhere in all of that, something probably landed for you — a spark, a frustration, a memory of a client you couldn't quite help the way you wanted to.

This exercise is for you. Not for your client file. Not for your supervising partner. For you.

Grab a pen or open your notetaking app.

1. Where did you almost lose your patience?

Think about a case, a system, or a process that has genuinely tested you. A referral that fell apart. A therapy waitlist that was six months long. A client who needed a therapist who spoke Gujarati and you couldn't find one.

2. What gap keeps showing up?

In your practice, your community, your client population — what is the thing that nobody seems to be solving? What do you find yourself explaining, apologizing for, or working around over and over again?

3. What resource would have changed everything in one of your cases?

It doesn't have to be realistic yet. Just name it.

4. What's one "can-do" move you could make in the next 30 days?

Not a five-year plan. Not a nonprofit. One email. One phone call to a local university. One conversation with a social work program director. One lunch with another attorney doing this work.

5. What's your biggest dream related to your immigration law practice? If you could wave a magic wand, what would it be?

Nobody starts this work with a full team, a field placement program, and a macro student producing infographics. I certainly didn't. I started with a phone, a client who needed help, and a stubbornness about not accepting that the gap couldn't be filled.

We are all in this together regardless of whether we work at a private firm or nonprofit or elsewhere. When we develop a vision for a better future and act on it, everything improves. Ideas and the money to accomplish those dreams will come to you in both expected and unexpected ways.

You're already a can-do kind of person. You picked up this book!

Conclusion

Ask anyone who has ever tried to end a phone call with me about a complicated case. I will find one more thing to say, one more angle to consider, one more hypothetical that starts with "but wait, what if—"

You have that instinct too, and now you have a better framework for asking more questions.

Maybe you handle family-based cases, or removal defense, or employment immigration. Maybe you stumbled onto a T visa situation and did not know what you were looking at. Maybe you knew exactly what you were looking at and just needed someone to walk you through the framework.

Wherever you started, you are not in the same place anymore.

You now understand the four pillars. You know how to screen. You recognize the industries, the patterns, the psychological architecture of coercion. You know that law enforcement certification is helpful but not required. You know that a bona fide determination can halt removal proceedings — and that when the system stalls, you have the litigation tools to sue. You know that a waiver exists for almost everything and that the bar for "impossible" in T visa practice is much higher than most attorneys think.

Most importantly, you know how to listen differently now.

That is the part that cannot be learned by only reading the INA. It is the instinct to pause when a client mentions their boss manages their travel documents. It is the discipline to say, "I think there is more to this — can we look deeper?"

The cases are out there. Survivors are sitting in your waiting room, presenting with what appear to be simple marriage cases, routine visa renewals, or standard removal hearings. They are the clients whose survival instincts make them answer your questions just a little too carefully.

You will recognize these situations. When you spot these subtle indicators, you have the framework to act.

This work can be hard and is also some of the most meaningful work I have done. I hope it becomes some of the most meaningful work you have ever done too.

For upcoming works in the T Visa Framework Series, see the https://mybook.to/Frameworkseries.

ABOUT THE AUTHOR

Connect with Helen on social media and get alerts about future books:

https://linktr.ee/HTLaw

Helen L. Tarokic, Esq., is an immigration attorney and owner of Helen Tarokic Law PLLC, a law firm based in Wilmington, North Carolina. She counsels both individuals and businesses across all areas of immigration law, including citizenship, humanitarian and victim visas, non-detained removal defense, employment and business immigration. She has practiced immigration law since August 2006 and is approaching 20 years as a North Carolina-licensed attorney.

Attorney Tarokic is a nationally recognized authority and legal strategist in T and U visa law. She teaches other attorneys to identify and advocate for trafficking survivors through webinars open not only to lawyers but also to social workers and law enforcement — because she believes that a multidisciplinary community is essential to securing justice and safety for survivors.

She is Board Certified in Immigration Law by the North Carolina State Bar's Board of Legal Specialization, a distinction held by only a small percentage of immigration practitioners in the state. Because immigration is federal law, she represents clients throughout the United States and abroad in their U.S. immigration matters and is admitted to practice in the North Carolina courts as well as the Federal District Court for the Middle District of North Carolina.

Attorney Tarokic has counseled clients in both English and Spanish since the beginning of her career. She developed her Spanish fluency through immersion programs in Taxco, Mexico, and Santiago, Chile, during her time at Lake Forest College.

As a first-generation American, she also speaks Croatian. Her practice also reflects significant commitment to Hindi-, Gujarati-, and Urdu-speaking clients as well, and she works with a team of interpreters to ensure that clients receive legal advice in the language they understand best, starting at the very first consultation.

She earned her J.D. from Wake Forest University School of Law in 2006, receiving awards for mentoring and for promoting the concerns of women in the legal profession. Mentorship from Professor Margaret Taylor at Wake Forest University School of Law connected her with key clerkship and associate opportunities. She moved to Wilmington, North Carolina, in 2008.

Before law school, she worked as a business immigration paralegal at Zulkie Partners LLC in Chicago from 2000 to 2003, where she developed a foundational knowledge of business immigration and temporary visas.

She graduated *summa cum laude* from Lake Forest College in 2000 with a B.A. in Psychology and a minor in International Relations. Her psychology background shaped the multi-step screening methodology she developed for her consultations.

She is a dual citizen of the United States and Croatia, and her family's own immigration history informs her ongoing advocacy.

Attorney Tarokic is currently a member of AILA (the American Immigration Lawyers Association) and ASISTA, a nonprofit that provides national leadership, training and support to attorneys to help enhance access to safety and justice for immigrant crime survivors.

Selected Writing and Media

- "T Nonimmigrant Visas: An Opportunity to Provide a Path Forward," AILA Think Immigration Blog, January 10, 2023 (co-authored with Attorney Jesse Bless)

- Interviewed for "CoastLine: Human Trafficking Victims Could Be In Nail Salons, Restaurants, Hotels," WHQR, November 30, 2018

Awards and Recognitions

- Elliot Ozment Award from Immigrants' List Civic Action, for making a positive impact on the immigrant community, June 19, 2026
- Selected to Super Lawyers, 2017–2026
- AILA National Sam Williamson Mentor Award, for mentoring immigration attorneys, 2018
- UNCW Community Partner Award for Excellence in University Engagement, 2016, for coordinating Spanish-speaking student volunteers to assist attorneys representing refugee mothers and children at the Dilley Detention Center
- Top Young Attorney in North Carolina Rising Stars, 2012–13 and 2015–16

Past Speaking Engagements

Attorney Tarokic has spoken at AILA national and regional conferences since 2008, on topics ranging from T visas and humanitarian relief to removal defense, H-1B practice, law practice management, and naturalization. She has served as both speaker and program coordinator for the AILA Carolinas Chapter Conference multiple times and presented at the AILA National and Regional Chapter Conferences, including AILA Philly and the AILA Central Florida Chapter. She has been a guest panelist at a Freedom Network conference and has spoken many times to students at UNCW, Wake Forest Law and other institutions of higher education.

Future Speaking Engagements

For structured private virtual law firm, law enforcement, or other organizational trainings; private "attorney brainstorm" consultations; and other options, please contact her via her website inquiry form at www.tarokiclaw.com. For matters outside her firm's scope, she provides referrals to a trusted network of advocates and colleagues.

Social Media and Events Platforms

You can follow her firm's updates on Facebook, YouTube, and Instagram, and she welcomes positive, supportive engagement with attorneys.

Continuing Legal Education

For Continuing Legal Education virtual and in-person programs, follow her on Eventbrite at https://www.eventbrite.com/o/helen-tarokic-law-pllc-13483453075 (or go to Eventbrite.com and look for Helen Tarokic Law PLLC).

Hosting an event?

Please let us know how we can help.

Acknowledgments

Writing this book while running an active law practice meant abandoning the idea of perfect timing. I wrote this because the information could not wait.

My husband and children are the reason I can do any of this: run a law practice, write a book, and teach CLEs. You are my home base.

To my team at Helen Tarokic Law PLLC, and to the collaborating attorneys, paralegals, social workers, and interpreters and others in the US, Croatia, Spain and India who make this work possible every single day: I could not do this without you. To Joseba Morales, professional illustrator and comic book artist of Gáldar, Spain, your ability to create art for difficult topics like trafficking or a pandemic, is so deeply appreciated. Thank you for bringing things to life.

My mother, Koraljka, a retired nurse, showed me that if a hospital doesn't have a botanical garden, you can just build one. Her dedication to a helping profession, and her optimism, are traits I admire. My father, Valentin, is no longer here to hold this book, and I feel that absence every time something worth celebrating happens. But his example is threaded through every page.

My sister Heidi deserves specific credit for the existence of this publication. Her can-do energy pushed this across the finish line when my schedule was threatening to bury it. When I say, "I don't know how," she says, "Yes and....?" knowing there is a solution.

Many thanks to Kate Burgess for her compassionate proofreading. Her old-fashioned English education in the 1970s and '80s resulted in someone with a wide vocabulary, well-versed in the intricacies of punctuation and grammar, and a fierce love of the Oxford comma. Any typos that remain, are solely my own.

Donusia Lipinski at Grace and Ease Life Coaching has cheered me on through more projects than I can count and has helped me implement systems to improve my health and wellbeing.

To the many attorneys who have created or guest-taught our CLEs over the years — you already know who you are, and so does everyone who learned from you. Thank you for preparing and sharing what you know. Thank you for showing up and being the community for new T visa lawyers who needed it so badly.

To the tremendous nonprofit advocates working to fill gaps, create resources, and drive impact litigation: thank you. I am grateful for Emma Buckthal, my original T visa mentor, and Namita Patel, without whom our Eventbrite programming would be unsustainable. Thank you to Rekha-Sharma Crawford, whose books for children facing immigration enforcement or trafficking inspire me to learn new ways to communicate and teach. Rekha's feedback on removal defense strategy, her work at AILA National, and her promotion of ethics programs has been invaluable.

To the professional law enforcement officers and prosecutors doing this work with integrity and care: you know who you are too. I'm leaving names out of this for reasons that have nothing to do with how much your work matters and everything to do with ongoing investigations. Keep going.

To the attorneys who called me when I was struggling, and to the ones who found the trafficking elements in a case before I did, and the ones who were nervous to file their first T visa and won after putting in the work: you are my inspiration.

To our attorneys, Katherine Haddock, Cory Sagduyu, Taiyyaba Qureshi, Isaiah Addair and Vanessa Reyes: you truly are a team and show up for one another and for our clients each day. Anna Lane Barfield and Luz Naranjo, you have been with me since the beginning. Your trust and daring to believe we will always make it through anything that comes our way make me a believer, too.

To my clients, the most remarkable people I know: You are not alone, and there are more wonderful people like you who deserve legal help all across the USA from attorneys who care.

A Note on the Limits of This Book

Everything in these pages is written for educational purposes only. Nothing here constitutes legal advice, and reading this book does not create an attorney-client relationship between you and me or anyone on my team.

The hypothetical clients you met throughout these chapters are fictional composites created for teaching purposes. They are not based on any single individual. Any resemblance to a real person's specific circumstances is coincidental. Real cases are far messier, more nuanced, and more human than any hypothetical can capture.

Immigration law changes. Regulations change. Agency interpretations evolve. Enforcement trends change. Court decisions reshape what we thought we knew. Sometimes, the spirit and intent of the law or regulation is not being implemented and must be challenged by advocates.

This book reflects my understanding of the law as of the time I wrote it, but by the time you read it, something may have changed. Verify everything. Check the current regulations. Read the latest policy guidance. Read the statute. Maintain a healthy skepticism. Question agency interpretations and remember that some of the most crucial elements of T visa practice are unwritten and require practical on-the-ground experience. Share your knowledge and your doubts. We build a stronger legal community by mentoring and supporting one another.

If you are a lawyer reading this to handle your first T visa, please reach out to a mentor, attend a CLE, and call someone who has done this before. If someone is too busy, find another person to team up with. I still look for people to team up with when I'm trying something challenging. T visa law, after decades, is a relatively new area of law because every few years there has been a new trend, revised regulation, guidance memo, or some other change to be reanalyzed.

You are not alone in this work. Neither are your clients. We all have our limitations, just like this book, but we can do better together.

www.ingramcontent.com/pod-product-compliance
Lightning Source LLC
LaVergne TN
LVHW052252200926
848481LV00002B/343